The Sportscaster's Notebook

by
Troy Kirby

All rights reserved
Copyright © 2008 by Troy Kirby
Cover Art copyright © 2008 by Troy Kirby
This book may not be reproduced in whole or in part, by computer or any other means, without permission.
ISBN 1438207204   EAN-13 9781438207209

Table of Contents

Chapter 1 - Hobby, Independent or Employee – Page 4

Chapter 2 - Finding Your Target Market – Page 9

Chapter 3 - One or Two Person Crew – Page 11

Chapter 4 - Advice for PBP – Page 17

Chapter 5 - Exercises for PBP – Page 27

Chapter 6 - Developing Your CA Skills – Page 55

Chapter 7 - Sports Talk Format – 59

Chapter 8 - Show Prep for Sportscasting – Page 70

Chapter 9 - Developing Your Writing Skills – Page 73

Chapter 10 - Developing A Sportscast Territory – Page 80

Chapter 11 - Selling Sponsorship – Page 86

Chapter 12 - Broadcast Equipment – Page 97

Chapter 13 - Developing A Commercial Log System – Page 101

Chapter 14 - Final Thoughts – Page 106

Index – Page 114

Cheat Sheet

This basically sums up a lot of the sportscasting theory used in this notebook. If you decide to read this and nothing else, it may help you a little. However, you will not develop your skills fully as sportscaster.

A show prep artist continually develops their craft.

Sportscasters have exceptional writing skills.

Read OUTLOUD to build LIVE copy reading skills.

Understand history and development of the game.

Sportscasters desire constant improvement.

Sportscasting means mistakes that you learn from.

Learn to practice from game tape to build skills.

Over-deliver for your sponsors.

Hit your target audience and do not ignore them.

You are not the show, only part of it.

Dress professional to be taken seriously.

Sportscasters know how to make the broadcast fun.

Do not speculate on injuries without confirmation.

Take your broadcast seriously, always.

Chapter One
Hobby, Independent, or Employee

In life, there are choices for every person. Always choices. This is one of the beauties of life, that no two people can experience exactly the same route to the same destination. Mainly because there are always different choices that people make along the way.

That being said, it is logical to assume that there are no similarities to every sportscaster's experience. No one calls the game the same way, and the games are even different. This makes things harder for those who want to learn, mainly because whom they wish to learn from will have a different experience than them.

Everything is always different, from the time, to the equipment, to the people that a sportscaster will run into on their way to their destination. Equipment changes with time, so does the voice of every announcer. Even the guys up in the big leagues have to work hard to improve their craft daily in order to continually fight off all of those young kids fighting for their jobs.

The primary concerns for any sportscaster will, however, be the same. How does someone get into the business? How does a person get on the air and start their career? How does someone stay on the air and improve their craft. While this book cannot answer every question, since no book can on any subject, it can help expand on the basic and advanced theory of sportscasting. By the end of this book, you should be able to develop your skills into a fully-functional sportscast.

The love of the game or the pursuit of an interesting career path will only go so far. Coachability is another factor. As a potential sportscaster, you have to kick your own tail to work hard, think faster, and develop the skills necessary in order to succeed. Otherwise, you wasted $20 on this book!

Those that think getting into sportscasting is easy are generally small market talents who never get farther than that first job, which they quit after a few shots at it. Some of this is mainly due to the vast majority of people, regardless of their talent level, not knowing how to get into the industry. That small market attitude stops a lot of people from moving on and moving up.

This notebook is meant to dispense with a lot of BS, mainly by preventing an avalanche of personal stories which do nothing for the reader and everything for the writer's ego. That being said, goofy stories about how someone got into the industry are not going to help you, the reader, get into the industry yourself. While those might be some really great stories or fascinating reads, if they serve little purpose, what good are they? Especially if your goal is become a sportscaster.

Even for the person who thinks that "I can do that" because they heard someone on the radio, this notebook can help improve your sportscasting from a hobby into a career. In order to develop those lines of learning, this notebook has been separated into various short paragraphs of interest. It is the writer's way of cutting to the chase. This notebook will focus primarily on the game of basketball and how to sportscast a game.

Basketball, with its quick rhythm and dynamic floor position, will allow a sportscaster to expand into other sports, such as baseball, hockey, volleyball and football.

Hobby

Some people will find pretty quickly that they have established too much time for other things, thus preventing them from having a full-fledged career in sportscasting. Do not let this discourage you from becoming a good sportscaster. If you want to do something, you can do it, within reason.

These hobbyists have spouses, children, mortgages, full-time jobs amounting to a successful living, and are too tied to the local community to be transplanting themselves every two years from team to team.

This is not a bad thing.

Often, people get into the industries like sportscasting believing that it is paved with riches, only to find that they are penniless within months and out of the industry within two years. The beauty of sportscasting is that if you need the "fix" calling games on the air, if you want to be a part of the action, you can do so, even on a limited basis. You will do it for the love of the game and probably enjoy it more than anyone in your family can imagine. However, if it is within you to be a sportscaster, but you cannot leave the wife and kids and travel 300 miles to the next minor league park, being a hobbyist is the next best thing.

Sportscasting as a hobby allows people to have the opportunity to remain in their local area, keep their steady job, and remain married without having their children taken from them by CPS. Most sportscasting hobbyists can find work at a recreation league or a summer AAU basketball tournament.

These positions pay nothing, and will cost sportscasters who simply want to do it for the love of the game. But the intangible of fun comes into play. Introduce yourself to the coaching staff prior to the game, prep a little, and take a handheld voice record along with you. Sportscasting can be a full-time hobby, one that you can pick up and drop at any time, if you don't mind the not getting paid part.

Independent

This type of position in sportscasting carries with it a lot of risk, and can be a marriage-killer and debt magnet if you do not know what you are doing.

Independent operators are mainly former broadcasters, who know the business, know specific sponsors who have a long-term relationship with them, and have a dedicated audience willing to follow their broadcasts anywhere.

The independent operator in sportscasting sets up the delivery method of the broadcast (terrestrial radio, satellite radio or internet), solicits sponsorships, and creates the entire broadcast, including advertising production, from scratch. If you miss a game, you do not get paid.

Although some people dream of doing this, the actuality of how much work for little pay hits as the reality of time commitment and effort take hold.

For every 30 second sponsor advertising on your broadcast, expect about 50-60 hours worth of work to solicit them.

This does not include the 100-200 hours of people saying that they are not interested or that they do not have it in the budget to sponsor your broadcast right now.

People arrive in the world of sportscasting expecting that it is a ton of money in the industry.

There is money in the industry, however, you probably will not see much of it.

If your goal is to be an independent operator, read the further in this chapter, especially the part about buying time.

Employee

You are the employee of a commercial radio station, athletic department or minor league team.

Commercial radio stations will likely have a lot of air shifts for you to do during the off-season.

Athletic departments may only contract you out at a $50 per game per diem.

Minor league teams may have you as a Director of Broadcasting, as well as selling tickets with a bonus system attached to it.

There are benefits to this position. The risk is lower. If the equipment breaks, it will be fixed.

After you have worked for a commercial radio station, athletic department or minor league team, you will have a professional name on your resume.

There are negatives to this position.

You will be paid little, sometimes without any benefits, and will be expected to work long hours for basically free.

You will pay for your own meals, travel and put up with a lot of input from people who really do not have a background in sportscasting (athletic directors, general managers and sports information directors).

Chapter Two
Finding Your Target Market

Defining a target market is a key principle of any business, and that includes sportscasting. How you position yourself as a sportscaster matters, especially if you are no speaking to your target market in general.

For instance, what if you decided to solicit sponsorship by expensive vacation resorts or luxury automobiles during a high school basketball tournament whose primary audience is low income families in a small residential neighborhood? You would likely miss your target audience and your sponsors would not sell anything because of it. Thus, a lose-lose situation exists. Sponsors need to see real dollars coming back to them, otherwise they will not sponsor your product a second time.

The first thing you need to do in order to pinpoint your target market is to see who you want to target. Let's say you are attempting to focus on a college basketball target market, which would likely be three targets (middle class families, men ages 24-35, men ages 55-65)

TARGET: Middle class families
SPONSORS: Real estate, banks, exercise gyms, dentists, hair dressers, clothing stores, fast food, restaurants.

TARGET: Men (age 25-35)
SPONSORS: Electronics, video games, potato chips, cars, casinos, movies, coffee, and alcohol.

TARGET: Men (ages 55-65)
SPONSORS: Luxury automotives, vacations, retirement communities, condos, golf courses, insurance, doctors, lawyers.

Notice that each sponsor has its own target market. This is due to the different interests of each target market. While men (ages 55-65) may be interested in condos, they are likely not interested in real estate as much as middle class families, who may be looking to move into a bigger home. And while middle class families may be interested in advertisements about restaurants, they may not be as interested in alcohol ads as men (ages 25-35).

This does not mean that you cannot have a sponsor which favors one target market over the other. However, if none of the sponsors you have are appealing to at least one of the target markets you have, it is a wasted sponsorship. If you have a mutual funds sponsor, but that appeals to men (ages 45-55) and they do not listen to your broadcast in enough numbers to matter, then you wasted the time of the sponsor, the listener, and defeated the purpose of your broadcast.

Chapter Three
One or Two Person Crew

Specific duties for both the play by play announcer (PBP) and color analyst (CA) are doled out when dealing with a two person operation. These are to keep the game flowing properly, without having consistent interruptions of people attempting to speak over one another. This involves the method of using non-verbal cues to alert each other when one is finished speaking so that the other can speak.

If a PBP is doing a solo broadcast, which may be the case for most of the sportscasters in the beginning, some of the details included in this notebook are good for review. A general rule for sportscasting, regardless of the size of the broadcast, is to essentially allow the listener to understand what is going on during the game. This means a steady stream of good information with a blend of detail and action.

As with anything that appears easy to do, a vast majority of the public likely views sportscasting as an easy operation. In this scenario, the PBP and CA arrive 10 minutes prior to the broadcast, links up with the radio station, broadcasts the game. Nothing could be further from the truth.

For every hour of sportscasting, you should be willing to spend about 5-6 hours of show prep work in order to make the broadcast sound smooth. A lot of people outside the industry would be shocked to see that estimation of time spent on the broadcast, until it was explained what exactly goes into show prepping for sportscasts. Part of this has to also do with prep between the PBP and CA, because the blend of voices and opinions needs to develop in harmony during the game itself.

Although a two person operation is easy, it will not fully develop your skills. If you are serious about honing your craft, performing a solo PBP sportscast is preferred.

Duties for a PBP

• The visual carrier of the mental picture for the listener. Knows names, scores, times, and positions. Understands how to convey each bit of information into a blended listening experience in which people may tune in and out in of the broadcast, yet still retain what is going on.

• Impartial (to a degree) in order to balance a color analyst or simply to convey the action to the listener. Doesn't try to out-scream or out-shout anyone, more interested in presenting details, even above the excitement of the play itself.

• Takes primary position while audio broadcasting and secondary position on video broadcasting.

• Gives score and time constantly during audio streaming, lightly on television where the score is visually shown.

• Seemless transitions between color analyst and game action.

• Independent voice, not attempting to give reasons for why action is happening, instead focusing on game flow. Details are important rather than why the play developed or was ran.

• Tries to be the voice of reason while sitting with color analyst, but uses questioning to color in order to lead color toward better developed answers during the broadcasts.

Duties for a CA

• Helps develop the listener's mental picture through verbal cues that enhance the broadcast.

• Gives reasoning behind each play (offense/defense) and why that method of play calling has been successful or unsuccessful against the opposition.

• Supports why a play occurred and gives predictions on what future play calling may occur.

• Analysis of what the coaches are telling the players and what is being said right now in order to correct any negatives in the game.

• Not an independent voice – supports the home team and tries to enhance the product of the game broadcast through analysis which is accurate and honest.

• Serves a secondary role on audio, a primary role on television.

• Knows when to shut up and doesn't relate everything back to their own experience, instead attempts to show the commonalities and insight of the game through intensive research and commentary.

• Not just a statistics reader, but illustrates a thought-processed voice of opinion.

Non-Verbal Communication

When you are working with a partner on the air, it is hard to let them know when you are talking and when they are supposed to speak.

The art of non-verbal communication is key to developing a good sportscast. Turning and looking at the partner, making eye contact, is the best way to let them know when you are ready to speak. It also allows them to know when they can shut up, etc.

A good balance of speaking can also be achieved through this method. If the PBP knows that they need to look at the CA every time that the ball gets into the basket, it helps cue the CA and allows the sportscast to ebb and flow correctly.

Non-Verbal Cues

• When the player with the ball crosses the half-court line, the play by play announcer takes over talking.

• When the ball is dropped in the basket, the play by play announcer finishes the play, then allows the color analyst to give further description or analysis.

• Let the color analyst be the main interviewer for halftime guests. Allow the play by play announcer to rest their voice.

• The Play by Play announcer should pose leading questions to the color analyst which allow the color analyst to open up about the game action and give it more detail.

Play by Play's Dual Role

The PBP has a dual role sometimes. The PBP usually is solo on high school and some college games, serving with a color analyst only when the big budgets come in. At other times, if the PBP can find someone to join them on the broadcast for free, it is a struggle to adapt to a new system of attempting to find form with new co-hosts.

There is a Hollywood actor who teaches a film class in Seattle without using cameras. The theory behind this is that camera work is a component of film, not the main artery of the entire system. The classes teach screenwriting mainly; how to develop more of your characters, of your scenes, how to show visual what the camera may not ordinarily pick up. The same is true for the sportscasting performed along with this book.

Forget about that special "phrase" or "cliché" that you came up with. Those are garbage lines meant to distract, not to enhance the way that people gain a mental picture from a verbal cue. Instead, focus on the poetry of how the game is flowing. Understand that each essence of how play is formed on the court is different from how you might be viewing it.

Keep in mind that you need to "set-up" the action as much as call it. Frequently, I heard the flow of the game being determined by the ball, which makes it seem like the NFL Draft – 2-3 hours of calling names. Instead, try to "blend" the broadcast by giving some details as to what might happen, who is open, who is being defended, who is coming into the game. This type of "blended" broadcast will create a mental picture from your verbal cues and allow the listener to feel an enhanced presence by what you say.

The PBP uses their eyes to describe each play, but how exactly does someone do that? Try borrowing game film from a coach or friend. Every coach has a ton of film and if they understand why you need it, they will likely give you a copy or two for free. It needs to be continuous, no different camera angle breaks, in order to help you understand and grasp the complexity of how to sportscast a basketball game.

With watching and calling game tapes, don't worry about reading the numbers, always seeing the score, etc. This is about building your skills. Just use generic names and be patient, this is a learning experience. You probably need to call about 4-5 games off of tape before you to prepared to call a live game properly, but everyone is different. Never call the same game twice, since your entire sportscasting career should be build on spontaneous calls.

Chapter Four
Advice for PBP

Personality – Your personality will develop as you build your sportscasting career. This takes time. Do not fake a personality in the hopes of "enlivening" a sportscasting when you are just starting out. In hockey, you have to learn how to skate prior to passing or shooting the puck. Learn the basics of sportscasting first, understand how to develop your skills further (even beyond this book!) and continue to build, build, build. The personality will come on its own and in fact be better than anything you could have dreamed up on your own.

Pronunciation – If you cannot pronounce their names, what in the hell are you doing in sportscasting? It is one of the most annoying things in the world to listen to; a sportscaster who says a name of a player wrong. It is worse if you are a parent at home, trying to listen in, and hear your family name mispronounced every time. In fact, its probably annoying enough for some parents to attempt to strangle you for doing it. Learn the names (you might want to ask the home and away coaches about the proper pronunciation of names during pregame warmups) and understand that everything is a balancing act.

The Art of the Over-Smile – Listeners to audio broadcasts cannot see you smile. In fact, if you do not attempt to "over-smile," you will sound monotone and unhappy. Part of the art of over-smiling, which has been used by everyone from telemarketers to radio broadcasts for decades, is to stare into the mirror at yourself. Call it "Joker Face" because you will look like Batman's arch villain, but do it and reap the rewards of non-monotone game calling. Practice over-smiling when you speak. The results will be drastic, but don't giggle when you over-smile.

Constants – There are specific constants in sportscasting which should be followed. Remember that you are the verbal carrier of the mental picture for every listener. *Time, Score, Teams, shot clock (with 9 or less to go), player fouls, team fouls, where are* *the teams are playing, timeouts each team has. This is especially true of time and score.* Those should be always on your mind regardless of whether the team is ahead or behind. It matters.

Less than 5 minutes in the half – Each possession in a basketball game gains in importance as the clock winds down. Depending on how the situation is carried our, one team may attempt more 3-point shots, try to run the shot clock down, consistently foul to send a player to the line, etc.

Game Flow – It is easy to get caught up in how fast the game is going. Players will toss the ball down the court or shoot quick shots rebounded and run down the other way. The beauty of audio sportscasting is how in charge the broadcaster is. You control what is seen and what is not seen. If the play on the court is going back and forth, verbally slow it down and describe each play. Unless you have a really bad memory, you should be able to recall what happened and how, then get back into the flow.

Don't just follow the ball - Often, one of the teams will attempt to "slow" the game after a certain point in order to gain their rhythm. This is the perfect time for you to describe off-the-ball movement (Example: *"Ellis is sitting on the outside of the arch waiting for the ball, fighting off Fields as the Rangers go into a 3-2 zone"*). Notice that this had nothing to do with the ball. Instead, this gave the anticipation that the player named Ellis might be doing something, that Fields might be able to steal the ball or defend him properly, that the Rangers are now changing their defense the suit the next offensive attack. This is why you were instructed to call.

Taking care of the voice – Save your voice for the big plays. Don't just call everything like it is the seventh game of the NBA playoffs with ten seconds to go in a tie game. Your voice may sound flat or monotone, especially when you are calling each and every play. Don't worry about it, your voice and ability will grow naturally as you progress. Most coaches usually take about 200-300 games before they are even considered developed. You aren't going to be any different. By calling as many games as you can, by developing yourself each day, you will grow into a sportscaster. How far you go depends on how much you continue to learn each day.

Lubricating the voice – Your voice is your tool, your meal ticket. Consider it like an engine, if you don't lubricate the engine with oil, it will burn up. The same will happen to your voice if you don't continually attempt to drink plenty of fluids. The best type of fluid for sportscasters is good ole H20 (aka water). Drinking soda pop or coffee might seem fine, but consider how much salt and other chemicals are in those drinks. Plus, they likely will make you belch or dry out your voice quicker than water. Aside from those reasons, water is also readily available and usually free. You will also have to regulate how much water or fluids you intake during the game, mainly because there isn't a bathroom break until the game is over.

Off The Court Action – Talking about what is happening off of the court can be tricky. It can be a part of the atmosphere of the basketball game (example: *Head Coach Antoni is upset with the call by the refs and kicking up a storm after that basket was taken away from his team*). But it can also distract from the actual game itself (example: *Head coach Antoni is hot right now. He's screaming up a storm at the ref. He just is letting the ref have it*). What exactly does that do for the listener? Is the game still going on? If the head coach is acting that way, is the ref reprimanding him? If so, what happened? If you call too much of the play by play off the court, you miss what is happening on the court. If the coach gets kicked out of the game, that is one thing. If the coach is just "jawing" at a ref and nothing is coming up it, all it creates is good theater. Unfortunately, theater is more visual than mental, therefore it distracts more than it helps your broadcast.

Reference Points – Audio broadcasts don't allow people to see anything, especially where something is. You have to verbally give the cue to develop the mental picture for the listener. Points as in how you see the call (did it happen to the left or right, did it happen on the top of the court or bottom?). These things matter in how you describe each play. (Example: *Wayne shoots a 15 foot jumper off* *the right side of the box which rims off left into the hands of Burl who turns and fires a chest-pass down to Canton on the opposite end of the court).* The amount of detail given here has dramatically increased the action in the mental picture that a person has of the play.

Working with a Board Operator – If you have the luxury of not being your own board operator, you will still need verbal cues in order to allow them to know when you are taking a break. (example: *We will be back right after this, 50-49 Bearcats up by one with 12 secs to go. You're listening to Ceni Basketball on KWJY News Talk 1000).* This type of example will allow your board operator to know when to cue an advertisement for a sponsor. SEE references for the <u>game commercial log</u> for more information.

Quick Recaps During the Game – If a team has gone on a 10-0 run, you need to give the audience a quick recap of what happened and why. Most listeners tune in and out, or do other things like folding laundry or drive while listening to sportscasts. Therefore it is crucial to give quick recaps of information as to what just went on. Image you are sitting at home and you hear that your team is down by 12, so you go take out the trash to satisfy your nagging wife. Then a few minutes later when you return, you hear that your team is only down by 2. What happened in this few minutes to make all of the difference? People want to know and it is just as important as the game itself.

Errors or Flubs – Everything has errors in it. This book probably does somewhere to. Even when its been rewritten about 5 times, every document could have a comma misplacement or a sentence that doesn't form correctly. The difference between you and a major sportscaster is the fact that the major sportscaster has about 500-1000 games under their belt. They have made most of the errors you will make, mainly because it is part of the process. Until you can call a game in your sleep (i.e. 500 games), it is understandable that you will make errors along the way. A comedian says the same material about 1,000 times prior to going up on stage and repeating it, just to make it *sound* spontaneous. Think of what you are doing as a sportscaster, you only get that chance once with a spur of the moment decision on how to make that call.

Spur of the Moment Interruptions – Expect the unexpected, even off of the court. You may get some guy who knocks off your headset. He may have done it by accident or just because he's a jerk. The trick is to ignore the problem, regain your composure as quickly as possible, call the rest of the game until a timeout or break occurs, then get someone nearby (athletic director, staff member) to take care of the problem for you. Getting you out of your game face is probably that guy's goal, mainly because he is jealous you are in a business he wants to be in. Never let a person get your goat.

Women vs. Men Playing – When sportscasting a game of women or men playing, the ultimate difference for you will be the speed involved. For a women's broadcast, you should attempt to have worked previously with tapes of men's games, calling them as best as you can. Then switch to a women's tape. You'll notice right away how easier you think it is to sportscast a women's game and you will likely perform better, faster. If you are going to call men's sports, I would suggest using a game tape of a higher level than the level you are calling (i.e. NBA tape for an NCAA game). Speed will still be an issue, but you will be able to catch up a lot quicker by adapting to the quickest speed first, then slowing down, rather than vise versa.

Things to say during free throws – Instead of just rattling off numbers, describe how the player is making the free throw. You can also use some of the personal information about the player (Example: ***"Gwen, a sociology major who was named student-athlete of the week back in December, crouches up with the first shot of this one-and-one free throw attempt which bounces off to the left of the rim, no good"***). Sometimes there is a long stretch of dead time in between a free throw, about 10-15 seconds where the floor is being mopped or a player is talking with her coach. You can use this opportunity to promote the next broadcast, give some upcoming schedule or team information.

Blue Language By Outside Forces – Sometimes a coach or a fan will curse up a storm on the sidelines or in the crowd, and your microphone will pick up all of it. There is nothing you can really do about this, and it happens to every sportscaster at least 20 times in their career. Either pot down the floor microphone, if you have on, or just attempt to cover your headset receiver with your hand when hearing this. However, if it is random or uncontrollable, just ignore it.

Eating During The Broadcast – Some sportscasters believe they can show up with a sandwich and eat it during the timeouts. This doesn't work and instead makes for a horrible audio broadcast. It also makes it more likely that the sportscaster will feel bloated or have to go to the bathroom. Don't fall into this trap; eat about 2 hours prior to game time. Your stomach and the listeners will thank you.

Fake Play By Play Southern Accents – They sound stupid, really. You may be able to fool some people with it, but really, you are making fun and offending an entire region of the country. And it sounds terrible.

Show prep prior to the game – A good rule of thumb on show prepping is to start about 24 hours prior to tip-off. Look up every stat imaginable on the team that you are playing, speak with your team's coaching staff and get inside details. Understand as much as you can about the team, about its next opponent, and about the season thus far. I would attempt to schedule a consistent meeting with the coaching staff the day prior the game (usually trying to schedule a day of game meeting with a coach doesn't work, for obvious reasons).

Interviews

One of the most important aspects of interviews is how to properly do it. Yes, there is a right and wrong way here. Ask open ended questions, not yes or no questions.

Mainly because if you ask a yes or no question, you get a yes or no question. One of the bad habits to break is the phrase "talk about..." which some reporters on-air attempt to ask.

This seems less about asking a question than filling time. Most of the interviewees asked this question seem more annoyed by it than actually answer it correctly.

Good questions to ask:

1. What happened in the last ten seconds of the game that turned the tide for you down the stretch?

2. How are you dealing with the loss tonight?

3. What are you doing to improve this season?

4. I noticed you changed the lineup tonight, why?

Bad questions to ask:

1. Did you like the game?

2. Does it feel good to win the game like this?

3. Are you going to win next week?

Interview Parrots

When interviewing players who are in high school or college, you have to understand that they are still kids.

Most of the time, they want to impress you and are willing to parrot back exactly what you say to them, because they really aren't thinking of the ramifications of what you are asking.

Most are thinking about their last date, Ipod, or what they are going to eat after the game.

With this in mind, be careful what you ask a high school or college player, typically they are not used to the media attention and could say anything.

Don't get them in trouble for absolutely no reason (if they didn't commit a crime, don't treat it like an interrogation), and realize that if they find it fun to be interviewed, more of their fellow players will do the same, and you can count on their parents and family to listen to your broadcasts.

A lot of what you can get a player to say can get them in trouble with their team, administrators, etc.

Keep this in mind when considering what questions you are going to ask.

An Interview Parrott Question:

1. Do you hate player so-and-so when you face their team?

2. Your coach yells a lot during the game, doesn't he?

3. You were pretty much the only one who could score tonight, weren't you?

Things To Know Prior to Tip-Off

1. Memorize the names of all of your team's players and coaches. Know them by sight.

2. Find out how exactly who the players are, know as much on their playing and personal background as you can.

3. Find out the little things going on with the team (not gossip, but details) which will help your sportscast sound professional and well-done.

4. Find last year's record, stats.

5. Search through a lot of newspaper records, see if there are articles or photos.

6. Everything you do for the home team, now do for the away team. Try to give your listener the most in-depth broadcast in order to help enliven the mental picture for them.

7. Know as much as you can about the opponent that your team is facing, as well as the next opponent after that. You should know who the opponent has played.

8. You should know what happened in the last two games for the both the home team and the away team. Know all of the nuisances of the season for both teams. This will increase your sportscast.

Things To Do Prior to Tip-Off

Arrange your notes in a show prep binder. Section each type of note into different subjects for easy access. Those subjects are:

1. Historical details on the team.

2. Stats of the season and last few games.

3. A roster sheet of home and away players, coaches.

4. Interesting details on individual players.

5. Stats of league standings and other teams.

6. Who, what, when, where, & how notes.

7. Give a pre and post introduction, wrapped around an introduction bed which allows you to flow into the sportscast.

Chapter Five
Exercises For Play By Play

Using game tapes borrowed from a friend or coach, call at least 3-5 plays of each of the following to create good theater and build-up for action as the listener is given an enhanced version of your sportscast.

A lot of people dismiss game tape calling because of the ability to rewind and repeat a call, while the action on the floor is spontaneous. However, the main argument against game tape calling when beginning in sportscasting does not hold up.

The main purpose is not to rewind and repeat the same call over and over again.

A person use game tapes to develop their sportscasts instead do so, if they are doing it properly, in order to their skills that otherwise happen too quickly in games to recall and develop.

Baseball players use game tape to watch pitch selection. Basketball players watch game tape to study their next opponent.

The purpose it is to select trends which may not be apparent to the naked eye without the advancement of film.

In the world of sports, everyone uses some type of recall method in order to develop their skills. Why should sportscasting be any different?

A word to the wise though - Use several different tapes when attempting to do a full sportscast. If you are isolating a play or developing a method for calling a foul or pass, then using a single game tape is fine. With a single game tape, you are not attempting to work in flow. You are being selective and attempting to learn to describe. If you attempt to use one game tape over and over again to practice a full sportscast, you will know what to expect from the game, and it will not help you.

Measuring the Shot

Know the dimensions of the court and how to use them in a sportscast by telling the listener where the ball was shot and how far away from the basket it was shot from.

High school court – 84 ft x 50 ft
College/pro court – 94 ft x 50 ft
Baseline to free throw line -19 ft
Width of the lane - 12 ft
Free throw line to backboard – 15 ft
College/High School 3pt line – 19.75 ft
Pro 3pt line – 23.75 ft

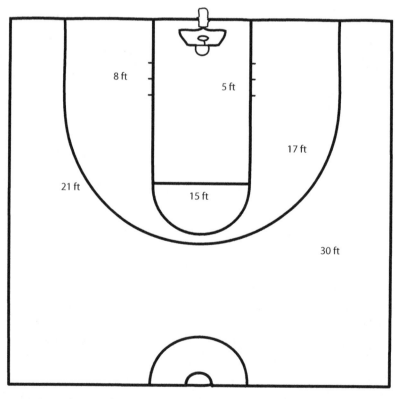

8 ft

5 ft

17 ft

21 ft

15 ft

30 ft

X you are here

Description

Describe the shot and the shooter?

1. Area on the court where the player took the shot. *Example: "Bobby off the left wing with the shot."*

2. Where did the ball land it did not go in the basket. *Example: "Ball pops up off of the left hand side of the rim and goes out of bounds."*

3. Did the ball hit the backboard? *Example: "The ball hits the top of the backboard's box and rims off down the left side."*

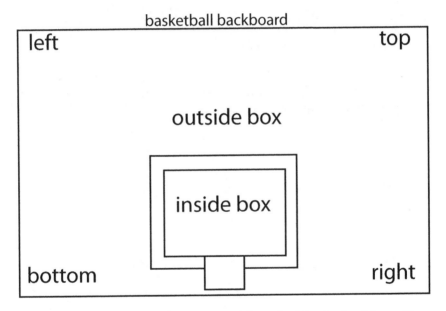

basketball backboard

4. Did the ball hit above, to a side or inside the backboard's box?

5. If the ball landed out of bounds – describe the baseline (are there letters spelling out the team's name? If so, on which letters did it land?) *Example: "Garrings' shot lands out of bounds, hitting near the A-L of the word FALCONS written across the baseline of the court."*

6. Did the ball land near one of the corners or near a fan?

    a.   What did the fan look like?

    b.   Where the cheerleaders nearby?

7. What if the shooter off-balance? *Example: "Simmons tosses up an awkward shot toward the basket with her right hand and twists like a pretzel."*

8. Did the shooter fall away or get pushed away after the shot? *Example: "Leslie gets hammered by two defenders after the shot is put up."*

9. How did the shooter land (on his back or stomach)? *Example: "Herr does a belly flop on the box."*

10. Was it an open shot or did the shooter have someone guarding him? *Example: "Yancy, double-teamed, still finds a way to get to the hole."*

11. How did the shooter get off the shot while being guarded (a juke move?)? *Example: "Jamal gets juked out of his shoes by Stevens who throws up a prayer."*

Segmenting the Court

The diagram below features a lot of different terms for the half court. This is to help you blend in a broadcast with more description and allow the listener not to feel they are being fed repetitive lines. The last thing that a sportscaster wants to do is bore an audience, because they usually tune out.

Feel free to add any lingo which you have in your verbal arsenal in order to develop the placing of each player on the court. The main point is to enhance, and this list is certainly not all of the different types of names for areas around the court.

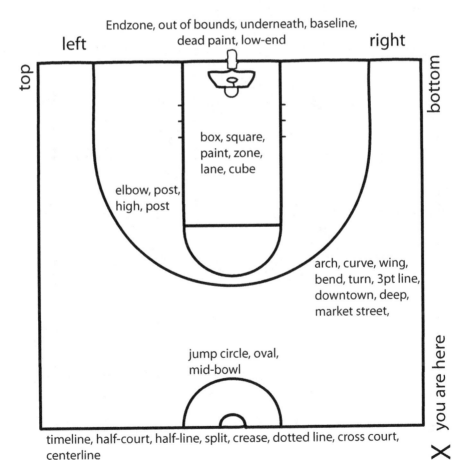

Exercise 1: Off-Ball Focus

Focus on a player who does not have the ball. If your intention is to create good theater, which a sportscaster is always attempting to do, then you need to develop your off-ball skills. This entails knowing where are the players on the floor who do not have the ball, but who can make the most impact on this play? What are they doing without the ball? Who is defending them/who are they defending? This primary reason for this is to heighten interest throughout the game for the listener, retain listenership numbers and progress the sportscast into a "must listen to" category.
Example: "Rider is being blocked out on the low end with his hands up, waiting for the pass inside the left end of the box as Stevens circles the arch with the ball. Rider cuts across to receive the pass from Stevens and lays it up and in."

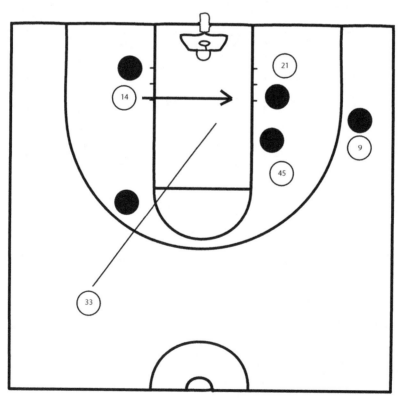

X you are here

Exercise 2: Non-Ball Action Focus

This is similar to the exercise on the last page, but now you will name the actions of every player on the court without the ball. Anytime they receive the ball, talk about everyone but them. This sets up anticipation of action happening and keeps the listener focused on your broadcast because everything is on the line at this point. If the listener only hears the tail-end of the play each time, they are not as emotionally invested as they are when every detail, including those without the ball, are talked about. *Example: "Henry keeps his defender behind him, waving his arms for the ball, then slips around the defender as the pass goes high his way."*

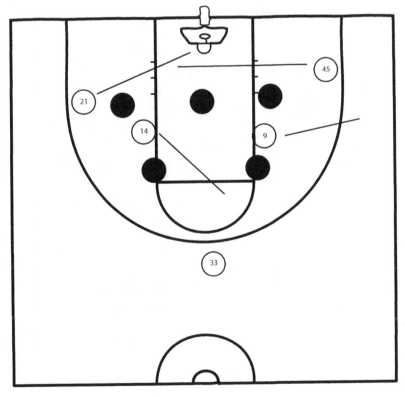

you are here

X

Exercise 3: Offense Focus

Another form of description is detailing how the offensive sets are being carried out by a team. You should look for what offense the team is setting into, whether they are driving forward with the ball or being pushed back by the defense. You should also be prepared to comment whether the team is keeping the ball on one side of the court or passing it throughout the key. Is one player acting as the leader of the team or are all of the players talking on the floor to each other. ***Example: "Crossing half-court, Jamison with the ball uses his right hand to decide a new play, showing three fingers high as the 2-1-2 zone applies too much pressure for the Devils do anything inside."***

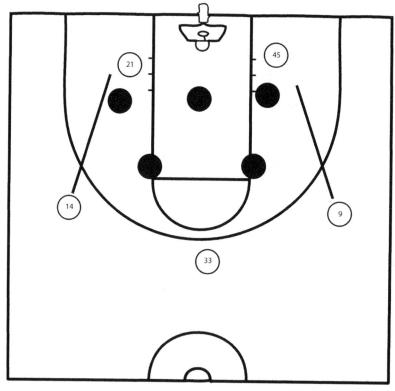

Exercise 4: Defense Focus

Talk about the entire defense being carried by out the team.
What defense are the opponents play and how is it effecting the
offense? You should also comment on who is playing out of
position and who is being double-teamed or triple-teamed. Who
is quicker than their opponent? Slower? This is especially helpful
when the offense tries to slow down the rhythm of the game. Your
listeners do not want to hear a sportscast that simply calls pass
after pass after pass as the offense moves the ball around the court.
*Example: "The Wave drop back into a 3-2 zone with Henderson
hiding on the right end of the box, working past the screen of
Dearborn as Garrison's point guard is being trapped over on the
top right corner."*

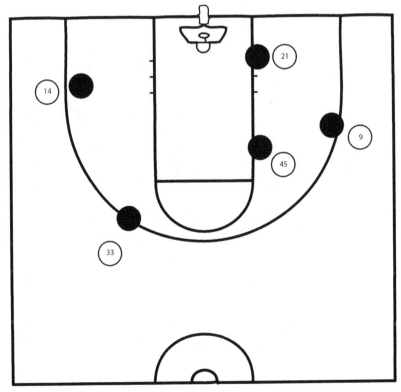

X you are here

Exercise 5: Shot Clock Focus

Focus on the shot clock as it winds down. After every description, mention the time left in the shot clock. This will enable you to refer to the desperation or great theater of every play, especially as the clock is nearing 10. This method can also be used for the end of the half or end of the game. It is best to wait until there are less than 2 minutes on the clock prior to making each shot sound like if it hits, then the game has been changed entirely.

Example: "Derring crosses the timeline with 21 on the shot clock. Baxter guarded by Steves waiting for the ball with Derring going cross court, 15 left. Henry moves through the lane as Derring passes to Baxter, 9 left on the clock. Baxter out to Henry, who passes it back to Derring in the corner. 4, 3, 2, Derring hits behind the arch in the bottom corner."

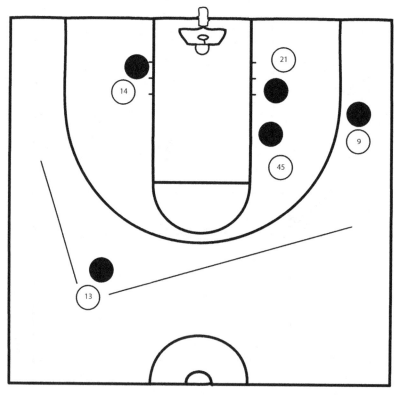

Travel Focus

Focus on any time of player travels with the basketball and describe it. Not just that they traveled with the basketball, anyone can do that. Instead, describe how they traveled. Did they slip on the floor? Did they walk with the basketball? Did they go up for the shot, then come back down without shooting? There are a lot of interesting ways that people travel.

Example: "Killenbeck into the top corner, slips and falls to his knees, turning over the basketball on the travel."

Dribbling Focus

Talk about how the player dribbles the ball. Is it between their legs? With a stutter step as if to drive to the basket? With a fake pass to the right, then a real pass to the left? *Example: "Wills uses the crossover to move past Derring and shifts off to the left side of the post, chest pass to Franklin all alone for the dunk."*

Pass Focus

Talk about how a person passes the ball. Do they pass from the chest? Do they pass using both hands? Just the right or left? *Example: "Fewing does a back turn to his right, bounces the ball off the court and into the hands of Derek who flips one over his defender right to Browning for the dunk."*

Foul Focus

Focus on a foul made by a player. How did it happen? Was the guy hacked or was it a bad call? Could you hear the foul from where you were sitting? Did he foul with his legs, his arms, his body? *Example: "Bowen drives to the lane and runs over Dereks, who gets the charge call as Bowen buried his knees in Dereks chest on the way up."*

Crowd Focus

Call the crowd: Give in detail what the crowd is doing and why they are doing it? Are they shouting, booing, crying, sneezing? Is it a zoo or are they quiet? *Example: "Probably one of the loudest school bands ever is playing tonight, blasting away as the students rock this joint silly after that dunk by Virgil to take a 10 point lead over St. Mary's."*

Coach Focus

Talk about what is the coach doing and follow the actions of the coaching staff? Are they agitated or calm? Are they making quick substitutions or merely responding to situations in the game? Are the players responding to the coaches, or ignoring them? How is the coach reacting the officiating? How is the coach reacting to a play that goes their way? How is the coach responding to a broken play? Is the coach standing in one place or walking the sideline? Describe what the coach is wearing, whether they are kneeling or standing, or sitting during the game. Do they shout plays or do they make hand gestures or do they cover their mouths with clip boards? *Example: "Coach Reed is hot under the collar after watching that dunk and turns to make sure the players on the bench know what went wrong with that defense."*

Building Focus

Look at the building: What about it is unique, what does the scoreboard look like? Is the ceiling low, are the lights bright or dim? Is there a blockade of signs (boosters, sponsors, etc) or is it vacant? *Example: "The Wooden Cage has been around since the 50s, if you can hear an annoying creaking sound in this broadcast, that's because they still have the same bleachers in place from the day they built it."*

Special Mention

Make sure that if you focus on the coach, crowd, building that it does not distract from the game itself. Make it blend in as added detail when the action is really off of the court, or in support of what happens on the court. Too much focus on the coach, crowd or building will distract from your main mission, sportscasting the game itself.

Sportscasting Notes for Baseball & Softball

Baseball & Softball sportscasting separates itself from basketball sportscasting in the method in which most people go about calling a game.

While basketball sportscasts tend to focus on memorization of names, uniforms through show prep, softball/baseball sportscasting tends to rely more on examining who the players and coaches are as individuals. What are their interests, their likes/dislikes and their backgrounds off of the field.

Know Your Listenership: Your listeners will be different from basketball to baseball to football to hockey to volleyball. It is best to try to come up with a specific audience that you are attempting to speak to. It helps you understand that if you are speaking to a stat geek, then stats are very important. If you believe that your audience is primarily casual listeners, then you might want to lay off too many stats, otherwise you will turn them off your broadcast.

Early Arrival: Get to the playing field within two hours prior to the game. This will give you time to hang around the pre-game practice, monitor what is happening, and speak with the coaches. Take notes and get as much new information as possible. Although the information off a website or from weekly notes is good, the happenings of information that day are more interesting.

Depends on the Coach: Some coaches can be tight-lipped and do not want their players disturbed during pre-game practice. Other coaches love the attention and let you talk to their players right up until the warm-ups are finished and the national anthem starts playing. Talk to the coach prior to speaking to any player, if they don't mind, then feel free to walk around and talk to players.

Be Responsible: Whatever you say in terms of what a player tells you matters. You may have caused a rift between them and another player, or you may hinder a contract issue with the player and team. It is good to find the interesting which sells the broadcast, but does not overwhelm it with controversy.

Be conversational: This should be looser than doing a basketball game. There is time to slooooow down. Let the game breathe, a little. At the same time, and at the risk of sounding contradictory, don't let there be too much dead-air if there are not a whole lot of fans in attendance or if those in attendance are making no noise. Hearing the crowd the crowd can be a scene-setter, but if there is no crowd, you don't need to step aside very often.

Tell Local Stories: Don't be afraid to tell stories, but do not use the major leagues as a crutch when you have nothing to say. If you have nothing to say about the play on the field, find something about the field, whether it's the dimensions, the grass, the sky. For example, what kind of grass is it? How is it mowed? What kind of clouds are those in the sky? One of the more interesting things someone might ever talk about in a baseball game they were calling in San Jose, North Dakota is the eagle nest that has been up on one of the light poles for decades! While other lights and poles have been replaced, that one has been left there.

Know Everything About the Pitchers: Learn as much as you can about the starting pitchers and the bullpens. They are at least 50 percent of the story. Perhaps a little less in softball (as compared to baseball) where starters will pitch for a longer percentage of the game.

Give the Score: Give the score, give the score, give the score, give the score, give the score, give the score, give the score, give the score, give the score, give the score... don't think you are giving it too much. Give it once a batter, at least. PLUS, think about another way to give it a few more times, like, with an egg timer, or minute glass.

Baseball Layout

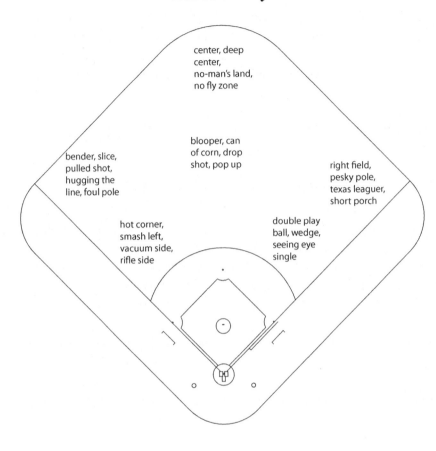

center, deep center, no-man's land, no fly zone

blooper, can of corn, drop shot, pop up

bender, slice, pulled shot, hugging the line, foul pole

right field, pesky pole, texas leaguer, short porch

hot corner, smash left, vacuum side, rifle side

double play ball, wedge, seeing eye single

Baseball Game Commercial Log

Date_____   Opponent _____

I hereby certify that the commercials listed aired at the times listed (name of announcer)_____ Date _____

Segment	Break #	Spot Title	Length	Client	Time Aired	Initial
1st Inning	#1	SPONSOR	:60	AD	_____	_____
2nd Inning	#2	SPONSOR	:30	AD	_____	_____
2nd Inning	#2	SPONSOR	:30	AD	_____	_____
3rd Inning	#3	SPONSOR	:30	AD	_____	_____
3rd Inning	#3	SPONSOR	:30	AD	_____	_____
4th Inning	#4	SPONSOR	:60	AD	_____	_____
5th Inning	#5	SPONSOR	:30	AD	_____	_____
5th Inning	#5	SPONSOR	:30	AD	_____	_____
6th Inning	#6	SPONSOR	:30	AD	_____	_____
6th Inning	#6	SPONSOR	:30	AD	_____	_____
7th Inning	#7	SPONSOR	:30	AD	_____	_____
7th Inning	#7	SPONSOR	:30	AD	_____	_____
8th Inning	#8	SPONSOR	:60	AD	_____	_____
9th Inning	#9	SPONSOR	:60	AD	_____	_____

Sportscasting Notes For Football

Football sportscasting is about the drive and thrill of excitement, more than the memorization of numbers or names. Usually, there are too many names to remember, that's why a good sportscaster at a football game will have an easy to read chart.

Aside from score and time, there are specific constants to each play which a good football sportscast will provide. They are done, frequently, in the following order of appearance.

1. **Position of the ball on the field** – At what yardage is the ball placed to begin the play? It is on the offensive or defensive end of the 50 yard line? Is it going left to right or right to left? Is it placed on the left or right hash mark?
Example: "Ball down at the left hash mark on the 34 yard line, waiting for the snap to begin as Berrington calls out his plays with a 10-7 lead in the first quarter with two minutes to go."

2. **Down and yardage for a first down** – Each play is worth a down of some type, either first down, second down, third down or fourth down. Football is based on the goal of getting 10 yards within four plays, therefore the yardage needed for another first down is crucial. This is important, so you had better say it each play for listener's benefit.
Example: "Second down and 3 on the Illinois City College 10."

3. **Offensive set** – What is the offense being called on the field?
Example: "Pro Set I Formation."

4. **Defensive set** – Most of the defense stays either in a 4-3 or 3-4 during the game, but there are times when the defense will switch to a nickel or dime package. *Example: "Defense goes from a 3-4 to a dime."*

5. **Motion of ball** – Is the ball thrown, fumbled, passes off or kept in by the quarterback? Is the ball tucked in or wobbled as it is thrown, is it a perfect spiral?
Example: "Jonah tosses a bad spiral to the halfback which

Stevens grabs and tucks under his arm as he goes into a minefield of Tumwater defenders."

6. **Offensive player with the ball** – Who has the ball after the quarterback? What does the offensive player with the ball do with it?
Example: "Henry grabs that pass out of the sky and runs down the endzone, juking two defenders as he crosses the 20, 15, the 10."

7. **End of play** – How is the play ending? Is the player stopped or do they score? On the what side of the endzone did they score?
Example: "Greg is brought down out of bounds at the 33 yard line of Baxter ."

8. **Defensive player with tackle** – The defense and who stops a play is just as important to the listener as the offensive side the play.
Example: "Simmons is sacked by Aaron, the middle linebacker just tore through the line and wrapped both hands around Simmons for the 10 yard loss on the sack."

9. **Yardage gained or lost** – Where the ball ends up and how much of the field is either gained or loss is important.
Example: "That play will cost the Diamondbacks 13 yards as Jennings runs up the middle on third down."

I Formation

WR · LT LG C RG RT TE · WR
QB
FB
HB

Slot I

WR · LG C RG RT TE · WR
LT
QB
FB

HB

Offset I

WR · LT LG C RG RT TE · WR
QB
FB
HB

Power I

WR · LT LG C RG RT TE
QB
FB · FB
HB

Split Backs Pro

WR · LT LG C RG RT TE
QB
WR
HB · FB

Wishbone

WR · LT LG C RG RT TE
QB
FB
HB · FB

Shotgun

WR · LT LG C RG RT TE
WR · WR
QB
HB

Wing T

WR · LT LG C RG RT TE
QB
WR
FB
HB

Offense

# First name Last name Height - weight - class Hometown (if college)	LT	LG	C	RG	RT

WR	QB	WR

SLOT	TB	FB / TE	SLOT

_____ Punter   _____ Place Kicker   _____ Long Snapper

_____   _____   _____

Quick Facts
Coach
Seasons coaching team
Records
0-0-0 and historical 0-0-0

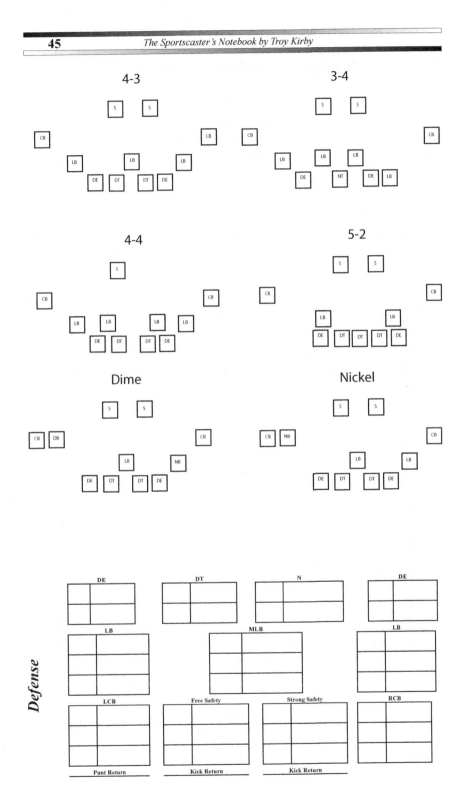

Sportscasting Notes For Hockey

Hockey is a mixture of football, baseball, volleyball and basketball in terms of sportscasting. While some of the names, locations, and movements are mentioned during a specific play, there is a continuity of flow which allows hockey sportscasting to blend with baseball's verbal poetry.

This may not seem like the initial sport to make this claim, however, as the game progresses with the small stalls in the action, there is a historical context which takes over the game in terms of how to sportscast hockey.

As with basketball, the ice is split up into several areas. This allows you to concentrate on memorization of the uniform numbers and player names. Some of this becomes tricky as teams have 30 players on each side. When in doubt, call out the number, then look and find who actually shot the puck.

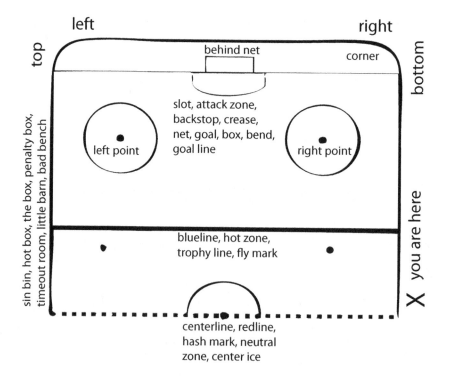

Example: Blue King's Stan Yellowman passes the puck across the center line to John Brike, who is checked by Deer Run's John Wilson, who steals the puck, brings it back on a breakaway toward the Blue King's goalie, John Abernaught. Wilson shoots the puck, but it hits the top of the goal and the play stops as Abernaught holds the puck. The lines will change and meet at the right point next to Abernaught's goal.

Example: "Yellowman to Brike at center. Brike checked by Wilson for Deer Run heading the other way toward Abernaught. Wilson fires, and hits crossbar. Abernaught will stop the play as the lines change for the face off at the right point."

If you noticed the quick succession in person to person (i.e. "Yellowman to Brike") rather than saying "Yellowman passes over to Brike on the left side of the ice," well, you are not alone in that. Hockey is a fast sport and typically the intermissions inbetween the periods are the only thing which keep the players from collapsing. Most players on a line play in a 45 second shift, meaning they are flying down the ice for less than a minute and then back onto the bench for the next shift.

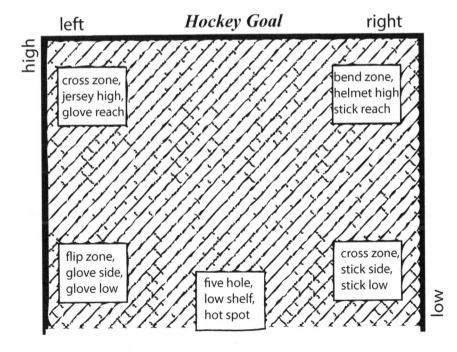

Hockey takes a tremendous amount of skill to pull off correctly in sportscasting. Not only do you have to have quick succession of relaying the most important information, but you also have to be able to remember all of the names that go with it.

One of the examples heard a lot of hockey broadcasts are the repetition of names in a machine gun format.

Example: "Yellowman to Brike, over to Abernaught, to Jones, to Brike, back to Yellowman in the corner. Brike SCORES."

Notice how little has been given to the listener. This provides the sportscast with next to nothing and could be done by some construction worker who was selected off of the street. Although it is tough to develop a fully-function hockey sportscast, the more detail you can provide, the better.

Part of this comes back to slowing down the game. Remember, no one can see the broadcast but you. This means that you can make it as long or as short as you need to.

Hockey, like basketball, has a lot of horns going off all of the time anyway. People cannot always tell one horn from the rest, therefore, even if you are 5 seconds behind a play and a player scores, continue on with your play by play until you reach the point in which that player scores. Do not rush the sportscast. Typically, you will be sitting in delay anyway for 5-10 seconds while the players parade around the ice celebrating, so you will need something to talk about.

At the end of the game, remember that hockey also has another feature: Three stars. A star is given to the top three performers (not always the home team solely) of the game. Even though this may sound stupid, it is something that hockey fans know about and what to hear. Some hockey teams encourage their fans to stay after the game, just to hear who got one of the three stars that night.

Hockey: 1st Period Commercial Log

Hockey Game Commercial Log - 1st Period
Date_____   Opponent _____
I hereby certify that the commercials listed aired at the times
listed (name of announcer)_____ Date _____

Segment	Break #	Spot Title	Length	Client	Time Aired	Initial
1st	#1	SPONSOR	:60	AD	_____	_____
1st	#2	SPONSOR	:30	AD	_____	_____
1st	#2	SPONSOR	:30	AD	_____	_____
1st	#3	SPONSOR	:30	AD	_____	_____
1st	#3	SPONSOR	:30	AD	_____	_____
1st	#4	SPONSOR	:60	AD	_____	_____
1st End	#5	SPONSOR	2:00	AD	_____	_____
1st Intermission	LIVE	1st Intermission	:20	LIVE	_____	_____
1st Intermission	TAPE	Station ID	:10	Inhouse	_____	_____
1st Intermission	LIVE	Recap 1st Period	2:00	LIVE	_____	_____
1st Intermission	#6	SPONSOR	:30	AD	_____	_____
1st Intermission	#6	SPONSOR	:60	AD	_____	_____
1st Intermission	TAPE	Feature on Player	2:00	Inhouse	_____	_____
1st Intermission	#7	SPONSOR	:30	AD	_____	_____
1st Intermission	#7	SPONSOR	:30	AD	_____	_____
1st Intermission	#7	SPONSOR	:30	AD	_____	_____
1st Intermission	#7	SPONSOR	:30	AD	_____	_____
1st Intermission	TAPE	Local Feature	2:00	Inhouse	_____	_____
1st Intermission	#8	SPONSOR	:60	AD	_____	_____
1st Intermission	#8	SPONSOR	:60	AD	_____	_____
1st Intermission	LIVE	Wrapup/Outlook	2:00	LIVE	_____	_____
1st Intermission	#9	SPONSOR	:60	AD	_____	_____
1st Intermission	#9	SPONSOR	:30	AD	_____	_____
1st Intermission	#9	SPONSOR	:30	AD	_____	_____
1st Intermission	TAPE	2nd Intro	:20	Inhouse	_____	_____
1st Intermission	TAPE	Station ID	:10	Inhouse	_____	_____

The first period log of hockey is rather a condensed version of an
entire basketball pre/post and 1st half log. Notice that everything
falls into place, into a pattern like that of basketball. Until you
reach the No. 5 break, which is a two minute primer. With this
break, you then head into 18 minutes of a post game show format.

Notice that there are taped portions of the 1st period intermission
which highlight a player feature and a local feature. In between
these are two LIVE segments to keep the listener updated with
the score. The two intermission period breaks are your bread and
butter of the broadcast, this is where you are going to make the
most money selling sponsorships. This is especially true if you
have listeners consistently tuning in during the breaks to hear all
about the period, how it unfolded, and what may be coming up in
the second half.

Hockey: 2nd/3rd Period Commercial Log

The second period log essentially matches the first period, with the exception of different features. This is mainly included in order to ease any reader's fears that somehow the second period was left off out of this notebook without any rhyme or reason. Same is true of the third period. Then, it goes directly into a short post game show.

Hockey Game Commercial Log - 2nd Period
Date_____   Opponent _____
I hereby certify that the commercials listed aired at the times
listed (name of announcer)_____ Date _____

Segment	Break #	Spot Title	Length	Client	Time Aired	Initial
2nd	#1	SPONSOR	:60	AD	_____	____
2nd	#2	SPONSOR	:30	AD	_____	____
2nd	#2	SPONSOR	:30	AD	_____	____
2nd	#3	SPONSOR	:30	AD	_____	____
2nd	#3	SPONSOR	:30	AD	_____	____
2nd	#4	SPONSOR	:60	AD	_____	____
2nd End	#5	SPONSOR	2:00	AD	_____	____
2nd Intermission	LIVE	1st Intermission	:20	LIVE	_____	____
2nd Intermission	TAPE	Station ID	:10	Inhouse	_____	____
2nd Intermission	LIVE	Recap 2nd Period	2:00	LIVE	_____	____
2nd Intermission	#6	SPONSOR	:30	AD	_____	____
2nd Intermission	#6	SPONSOR	:60	AD	_____	____
2nd Intermission	TAPE	Fan of the Game	2:00	Inhouse	_____	____
2nd Intermission	#7	SPONSOR	:30	AD	_____	____
2nd Intermission	#7	SPONSOR	:30	AD	_____	____
2nd Intermission	#7	SPONSOR	:30	AD	_____	____
2nd Intermission	#7	SPONSOR	:30	AD	_____	____
2nd Intermission	TAPE	Game Promotion	2:00	Inhouse	_____	____
2nd Intermission	#8	SPONSOR	:60	AD	_____	____
2nd Intermission	#8	SPONSOR	:60	AD	_____	____
2nd Intermission	LIVE	Wrapup/Outlook	2:00	LIVE	_____	____
2nd Intermission	#9	SPONSOR	:60	AD	_____	____
2nd Intermission	#9	SPONSOR	:30	AD	_____	____
2nd Intermission	#9	SPONSOR	:30	AD	_____	____
2nd Intermission	TAPE	2nd Intro	:20	Inhouse	_____	____
2nd Intermission	TAPE	Station ID	:10	Inhouse	_____	____

Hockey Game Commercial Log - 3rd Period
Date_____   Opponent _____
I hereby certify that the commercials listed aired at the times
listed (name of announcer)_____ Date _____

Segment	Break #	Spot Title	Length	Client	Time Aired	Initial
3rd	#1	SPONSOR	:60	AD	_____	____
3rd	#2	SPONSOR	:30	AD	_____	____
3rd	#2	SPONSOR	:30	AD	_____	____
3rd	#3	SPONSOR	:30	AD	_____	____
3rd	#3	SPONSOR	:30	AD	_____	____
3rd	#4	SPONSOR	:60	AD	_____	____
3rd End	#5	SPONSOR	2:00	AD	_____	____

Sportscasting Notes For Volleyball

Sportscasting for volleyball matches is intense and different that even those fast-paced games such as hockey or basketball. The intensity comes from quick-rotations, hammering swings, and the score rapidly changing via a point being awarded every time. In order to offer the best audio broadcast possible for volleyball, you must be intent on knowing the game itself calling the motion of the ball, the player names, and keep up with the action.

Example: Titans versus Rainbows
The Titans Beau served the ball into play and the description of the serve was called. The ball went over the net to Arron, who received it and hit it up for Wae to serve. Wae's serve was attacked by Stephens who hit the ball back over the net into Titans defense, hitting off of the Titan's blockers and scored a point for Rainbows.

Example play call: "Titans Beau sends across a jump floater to Arron, to Wae, for Stephens plays a heavy swing off the block for the point, 1-0 Rainbows."

The principle of this basic volleyball play calling is to determine who serves the ball, who receives it, and how does the play continue or end. It is not necessary to always call a dig, a set upon reception, or the attack. These are common enough that if they do not add to the broadcast, they stretch the amount of description you give during the play, thus you may miss something as volleyball's speed really kicks up with every point.

During every reset, when there is a timeout on the court, you should always come back with a mention of the rotation for each side, naming off each of the players and which position they are in. The clock itself is unimportant, however the score is. Name the score after each point and only the match score when the game score is nearing match point.

Where the ball lands is not as important as how the ball was played. However, if you feel you can describe this information post-play, it will add to the value of the listeners' mental picture.

There are several different ways to describe the motion of the ball which will help you break down and isolate each player's actions if necessary.

Ball Crossing The Net Descriptions
"Sends it across" – "Brings it back" – "Floater" – "Pushes it back over" – "Stays alive over the net" – "Joust over the net" – "Clears the net"

Ball Being Received From Attack or Serve
"Keeps it up" – "Brings it back" – "Going for the push" – "Sends it up" – "Roll shot" – "Handled by" – "Plays it off the line"

Ball Being Defended From Attack or Serve
"Off the block" – "Misses the block" – "Passed back to" – "Backrow to" – "Off the scramble" – "Backrow for ball" – "Dives to keep it alive" – "Second timer"- "Backrow ball" – "Blocked but keeps it over"

Ball Being Set For An Attack
"Going to set it up" – "Rolls it over" – "Quiet off the set" – "Tosses a floater" – "Sets up for" – "Goes to the outside"

Ball Being Attacked
"Gets a swing" – "Gets another crack at it" – "Hits slide right" – "Leaps and kills it" – "Pumps and jumps" – "Hits it low" - "Going for the swing" – "Unloads another" – "Has a heavy swing" – "Comes out of the back row to hit"

Ball Attacked Successfully
"Off the hands" – "Out of bounds" – "Hits the tape" – "Wipes off the block" – "Ball goes long" - Can't handle it" – "Loses it off the line"

Volleyball: Commercial Log

With volleyball, there are fewer timeouts, but that can be a blessing in disguise as it makes inventory of your best spots limited, those you can charge more for them. In each game, you will have two 60 second spots.

At the end of games 1,3,4 there is a two minute intermission commercial break. At the end of game 2, there is a 10 minute break. This is primetime real estate for any sponsor and those spots should sell the highest.

If you notice that there is a sort of mini halftime show in between games 2-3 to cover some of the time.

Volleyball Game Commercial Log

Date_____   Opponent _____

I hereby certify that the commercials listed aired at the times listed (name of announcer)_____ Date _____

Segment	Break #	Spot Title	Length	Client	Time Aired	Initial
1st Game	#1	**SPONSOR**	:60	**AD**	_____	_____
1st Game	#2	**SPONSOR**	:60	**AD**	_____	_____
1st End	#3	**SPONSOR**	2:00	**AD**	_____	_____
2nd Game	#4	**SPONSOR**	:60	**AD**	_____	_____
2nd Game	#5	**SPONSOR**	:60	**AD**	_____	_____
2nd End	#6	**SPONSOR**	2:00	**AD**	_____	_____
Mid 2-3	LIVE	Recap	3:00	Inhouse	_____	_____
Mid 2-3	#7	**SPONSOR**	:60	**AD**	_____	_____
Mid 2-3	TAPE	Player Highlight	2:00	Inhouse	_____	_____
Mid 2-3	LIVE	Wrap/Intro	:60	Inhouse	_____	_____
3rd Game	#8	**SPONSOR**	2:00	**AD**	_____	_____
3rd Game	#9	**SPONSOR**	:60	**AD**	_____	_____
3rd Game	#10	**SPONSOR**	:60	**AD**	_____	_____
4th Game	#11	**SPONSOR**	:60	**AD**	_____	_____
4th Game	#12	**SPONSOR**	:60	**AD**	_____	_____
4th End	#13	**SPONSOR**	2:00	**AD**	_____	_____
5th Game	#14	**SPONSOR**	:60	**AD**	_____	_____
5th Game	#15	**SPONSOR**	:60	**AD**	_____	_____
5th End	#16	**SPONSOR**	2:00	**AD**	_____	_____

Volleyball Court Locations

During the play action, the location of where the ball landed will probably be the least of your concerns. The quickness with which a play with happen and interact with the players involved, will give you enough to worry about. However, one of the benefits of sub outs and the stoppage of play after the point prior to the next serve is that you can split up the court and recall the location of where the ball landed.

In the diagram below, one half of a volleyball court is shown. It is split up to illustrate an easy reference system in which every ball landing hits a specific location on the court. This should help as you recall a play, giving a short analysis of each attack and how it was defended.

Example: "Browning took the serve to the outside right for Keri whose swing landed on the back center of the court in between the block for the point."

Front High	Front Center	Front Low
Back High	Back Center	Back Low

Chapter Six
Developing Your CA skills

Blowouts – It is unnecessary to tell your listeners that a blowout has happened, especially too early in the game. Why? Because you have an obligation to sponsors and the teams to attempt to "hold" those listeners for most if not all of the game. If you do say it's a blowout, it better be at the end of the game in order to gravitate the situation further in the listener's mind. Don't make fun of another team in a blowout, instead, attempt to be creative and talk about who the next opponent is, give some good examples of what the losing team did (if any), and what concerns the team needs to address. The last thing you want to say is: *"it's the first quarter and this game is over,"* mainly because your listeners will tune out and your sponsors will be upset with the result.

Amateur vs. Pro Rule – Being a player who is criticized by the on-air person sucks. Especially if you are an amateur (i.e. High school, college, rec league, lowest minor league). The fact is, a player at that level is trying their hardest, playing the game without seeking compensation, as is in many ways, learning, just like you are. There is a BIG difference between being an amateur and being a pro, one of them is the criticism you receive. Plus, at the lowest level, if you criticize some high school kid, their parent might listen. A few things that can happen to you if you offend a parent: Loss of sponsorship, loss of broadcasting right to the games (the PTA might pull the plug on you) and loss of life (parents are nuts anyway, why antagonize them?).

Knowledge – Attempting to "wing" a broadcast is a recipe for disaster, especially if you are serious about attempting to develop yourself as a sportscaster. Imagine if the players on the court did not practice, or slacked off practicing. How good would those players be in game action? Being "lucky" in a broadcast doesn't mean you are prepared. So start "show prepping."

Officiating – Referees are usually some of the best and worst of the sport. Mainly due to who you root for and what happens in the game. People are human. Therefore, you shouldn't attempt to ride the refs when they make bad calls. You can mention it, you can come back to it if the play really turned the tide in the victory, but don't keep focusing on it. Listeners want to hear about the action, not a running commentary on something that may or may not make the newspapers the next day. Besides that, you don't want to look like a homer, instead, try to look homespun.

Homer vs. Homespun – Some sportscasters attempt to really be in the thick of things and call everything as if the world is against their team. This is not professional and in fact, can backfire on the sportscaster. Saying things on the air like *"We got screwed by the refs"* or *"They aren't calling fouls on so-and-so"* is not classy. Remember that half of your audience might be the opponent's fans. They deserve to hear a good broadcast, even one which originates for the other team, rather than just a homer sportscast where everything can't be trusted. Being homespun means that you know the game, call the details of it accordingly, and happen to be interested more in the excitement of your team doing well rather than the other guy.

Know the game – This is one of the things that sounds easy, but takes a lot of work. Know each of the calls by the refs, why they are making those calls, what offenses and defenses are being made by the teams, and why substitutions are being made. Simply assuming makes you look like an amateur.

Calling out a player or coach on the air – While it may seem like you are doing "what sports is all about" but calling out a player or coach is stupid. First, the players are likely trying as hard as they can, and you may be offending someone by your comments (especially if they are student-athletes). Second, calling out a coach is stupid. It may get you punched or kicked out of the gym or off that school/team's broadcasts for good. Why? Because coaches know, may be friends with, or may just have a general respect for one another. A single listener can destroy your gig or at least make your life a living help by destroying your relationship with your own team.

Don't Say What Any Turkey Could – You need to give in-depth analysis, not retreated crap you've heard on ESPN or Fox Sports. This means being learning how each team runs a play, which plays they favor, the offensive and defensive schemes, and presenting a mental picture of each through verbal cues. Don't just say that a team is running an "3-2 defense," describe it to the listener at least once per game, tell them exactly why a team would do that in order to defend the basket.

Don't Speculate On Injuries

You are not a doctor.

Repeat, you are not a doctor.

Unless you have been to school for 7 years. Unless you have a medical license and have performed open heart or Tommy John surgery, you are not a doctor.

If you are a doctor, even then, you should not speculate on a possible injury during the sportscast in which the injury occurs.

Too much is made of injuries anyway.

If you have an injury confirmed by an athletic trainer, and it has been announced publicly, then use your discretion.

Reason #1 - If you are sportscasting a high school or college game, you might frighten a parent who is listening at home. This may cause you more grief than you want and may get people less likely to have you on the air.

Reason #2 - If the injury looks serious, but isn't, you look like a fool. That basketball player who looked like he broke his leg and stumbled off to the locker room in the first half, but then ends up returning in the second half, scoring 40 points just made you look as if you don't know what you are talking about.

Chapter Seven
Sports Talk Format

In the late 1980s, the format of Sports Talk shot through the world of radio as the next big thing. Although the format has seen its ups and downs, it has survived to some extend. This chapter should help you attempt to navigate the format successfully. It is written more as its own primer of advice, since, aside from the topic tree, there are really no extensive exercises to perform.

The goal of any sports talk show is to get the listeners to continue to listen through each quarter break (15, 30, 45, 00). This is how each station divides up its ratings from the highest levels to the lowest levels of the industry. It is also how stations sell commercial advertising, so hitting that target audience and retaining it through the quarter break is crucial to survival on any station.

An example would be that most sports talk listeners are not interested in listening to a show about the latest bill going through Congress. Unless that bill is directly involved in sports (stadium, beer sales, limiting eligibility of high school athletes, antitrust). While some of that talk may be permitted, assume that the more a sports talk format announcer talks non-sports, the less audience they have. While sports talk listeners are typically some of the most loyal, segmented audience in all of radio, they will tune out if they are not continually being catered to. So talk sports!

It is important to remember that callers typically make up less than 2 percent of the listening audience. Most are casual fans who want to get away from the worries of the day and concern themselves with something trivial which will not mean a life or death result. That is why talking about serious subjects is not advised (unless a local or national tragedy just happened – see 9/11).

Format: Single Announcer

This is the one most popular of all of the formats in sports talk. It usually comprises of a single announcer who takes calls on a 5 second delay system. The caller starts each hour of the show with one primary and two secondary subjects for the first 13 minutes, then allows the callers to digest each subject with a break. This allows the callers to "fill up the phone lines" prior to coming back to the single announcer.

Format: Dual Announcers

This format tends to go away from callers, instead relying on show prep and guests in order to fill the void of each hour. The dual announcers tease each quarter break with another subject, mentioning it in order to keep listeners "hooked" as the show progresses. While there are some callers, the format tends to shy away from letting the listeners voice their opinion, staying mainly with the dual announcers as the opinions for the show.

Format: Forum

This format stays away from callers entirely until it is determined that a "call-in" segment is being initiated. This call-in segment lasts usually for five or less total callers per hour and allows the forum, made up of experts in the field (or journalists who think they are experts in the field!) to become wisdom providers to the audience. This is not a bad format, but one in which cannot be sustained daily for five days a week.

Producing: Where it starts

If you want to be at a sports talk station, you may end up being a producer prior to being the talent. There are too many people in front of the microphone typically, and a station needs producers. A producer is the behind the scenes person who manufactures the guests for the talent, works on show prep, helps blend topics, records or plays highlight or interview clips, and screens callers to ensure that there is quality with the calls. Producing is a tough, thankless, a what-have-you-done-for-me-lately job that everyone needs but no one really understands.

Producing: Guest Calling

If you performed telemarketing back in high school, this is the closest thing to it. Not only do you have to sell the guest on the fact that they should be on your show, you have to arrange a time in which they need to either call back into your station or that you can call them. This also needs to be coupled with the fact that the talent needs to be ready for the guest, that the previous guest or callers may have gone over in time, or that the guest simply forgot to call back in or is now too busy to come on the air. Guest calling can be fun, as long as you do not get star struck if you get that guy to go on the air that struck out 10 batters last night.

Rule 1: Be professional and courteous. Tell them what the topic of the show is about. Do not attempt to ambush them or it will get around in the sports community and no one will come on your show again.

Rule 2: Find a time that works for both you and the guest. If you have a morning show and need the interview on at 6:30 a.m., you may have to record the guest in the afternoon the day before in order to get them on the air. Understand that you are not the only person demanding of their time.

Rule 3: Make sure that that you have enough show prep on the guest for the talent. Some talent end up doing a lot of show prep. Others are small market jerks who show up at the station and wait to be handed something. The worst radio ever is an interview in which the talent knows nothing about the guest, which happens. Your job is to make sure that does not happen.

Rule 4: If something happens, be flexible. Have a backup plan of additional show prep or another segment in order to make up for the fact that the guest could not make the show, etc.

Producing: Highlight Clips

The best highlight clips have relevance back to a story segment and last less than 2 minutes. Simply finding every homerun call to place into a highlight clip does nothing for the listener or for the show. You have to continually think about what makes every highlight interesting in that clip. Imagine if there were a highlight clip full of play by play every time a batter walked or something mundane. That is what continual homerun calls sound like when placed together. Make your highlight clips interesting. Every game has more than one story and your job is to find it in a highlight clip.

Producing: Interview Clips

An entire press conference is great for listeners who want to log onto your website and download the entire three hour interview clip, complete with reporters questions and the interviewees lame jokes. Instead of simply being a record and broadcast producer, you need to cut the interview to the heart of the story. What happened that makes this interview interesting? Specifically, what answers did the interviewee give which will make the listener turn up their car radio volume in order to hear it? If an interview is boring, you are losing listeners by playing it. Coach press conferences are only interesting if you cut them to focus on the most important answers regarding the team, not the answers that are throwaways.

Producing: Segment Creation

The talent has a lot of say in daily and weekly meetings about segment creation, however, they typically focus on the larger issues for each show rather than each quarter hour. Segment creation, every quarter hour of a 4-to-5 hour show, usually falls in the producer's lap. Segment creations means talking a mixed salad approach to the show. Simply allowing the talent to "throw open" the phone lines does nothing for the show and exposes the show to the danger of having less and less people call.

SEGMENT CREATION: 12 p.m. - 1 p.m.

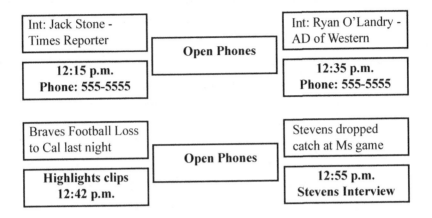

Producing: Blending Topics

Part of producing a good show is understanding that the more you continually speak on one topic, the less audience you have. Remember that you have soccer, football, basketball, baseball, hockey, golf, tennis, and every other sports fan imaginable listening to your program. That being said, talking five hours of golf every day will likely get you a reprimand from the boss rather than a raise. Blend the topics of golf and football and baseball and hockey. The more you stick primarily to one topic, the less audience you have. Every sport has some type of value, your job is to hit that target audience and expand upon that value so that they listen through every quarter hour, even when they are a football fan and you are discussing a topic (such as golf) that they do not really care about because they are sure that in the next segment, you will be talking about football.

Producing: Feeding Callers

Part of the dirty little secret of call screening is that some producers prep their callers more than the general listening audience knows. Some producers are lazy and simply ask you what topic you want to talk about. Other producers get the topic you want to talk about, then discuss it with you, honing your call until it is something that

Sports Talk Topic Tree

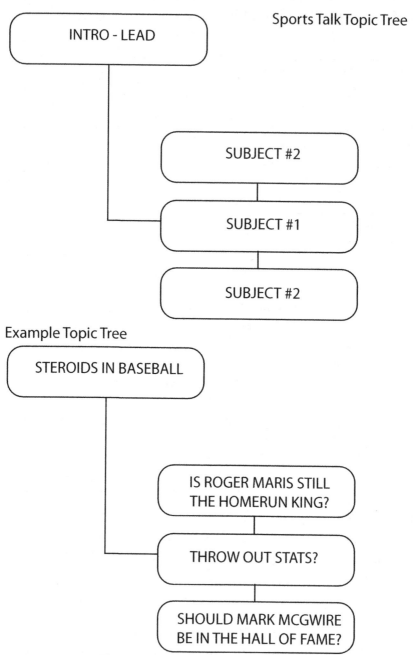

INTRO - LEAD

SUBJECT #2

SUBJECT #1

SUBJECT #2

Example Topic Tree

STEROIDS IN BASEBALL

IS ROGER MARIS STILL THE HOMERUN KING?

THROW OUT STATS?

SHOULD MARK MCGWIRE BE IN THE HALL OF FAME?

This tree example shows how one basic topic can spawn into several different thoughts on the same subject. The purpose is to help a host when a topic gets hot continue to keep the conversation going into different directions and keep the listeners interested.

the talent can really discuss on the air. Remember that on-air is expensive and valuable real estate. Sometimes you have to work out the bugs of a caller in order to get that gem from them on the air. Some thoughts on call screening include telling them to be energetic, concise, telling them that they need to work on their points and shoot them a few points to rattle off on the air.

Example

Producer: Station KWIW Sports Talk?

Caller: Hi, this Jerold, I want to talk with announcer on the air.

Producer: What's your subject?

Caller: I want to talk about the basketball team's record.

Producer: What's wrong with their record?

Caller: They are 10-23!

Producer: Yes, but how would you change the team?

Caller: I would fire the coach and GM for starters.

Producer: So, you really want to talk about firing the coach and GM.

Caller: Well, yeah, I mean, we do not even run good plays and I think we are not practicing enough on the defensive end of the court.

Producer: You mean how we have lost our last five ball games by 20 points or more.

Caller: Yeah.

Producer: Well, make sure you say that so our listeners know, okay? You'll be up next after the break.

Notice that the producer focused the caller's subject. First, it was about the team's record which seems generic enough. Then, it was about firing the coach and GM. Instead of being satisfied, the producer continued to focus the caller until it came out that the caller really wanted to talk about the team's lack of defensive. The producer then fed the caller a statistic to make the caller's argument appear to have merit to the listening audience and reminder the caller that what he was saying would be heard by the listening audience. Yes, the producer fed the caller. Yes, the caller's argument is not spontaneous. But, so what? The sports talk format is entertainment. Callers who are uninteresting are not entertaining, they are boring.

Producing: Handling The Talent

Small market radio or television talent is the worst. They are typically frustrated people who spend their life consumed with anger because they did not make it to the big time. They are also people who cannot help but be consumed with every little detail of mismanagement. They also enter the building late, they do not show prep, they road block your ideas, and they "wing it" whenever they chose to, which is likely often. The best way to handle talent is to do the best that you can, then move on. Leave the talent behind. Do not repeat their mistakes, which typically come from others who have told them that there is no money in the business and that their crappy attitude is acceptable. That is why they are in small market entertainment. If your goal is to be in big market entertainment, you need to be patient and avoid being like the talent who are stuck in small markets.

Producing: Daily/Weekly Show Meetings

These meetings are designed to go over the basics of each show. Some talent are more interested than others in having meetings. The more prepared everyone is, the better it is for the show. A daily meeting lasts about 10-15 minutes and is held about an hour prior to the show's broadcast. This brief overview meeting is to go over who the guests are, what the topics are going to be discussed, and to hand whatever show prep the talent needs to them. The weekly meetings are usually held on a Monday, about two hours prior to the show, last about 30-45 minutes, and allow both the talent and the producer to talk through any issues they felt came up during last week's shows. Meetings are the only way to fully prepare for the shows and improve the show's quality.

Producing: Live Remotes

Some of the worst sports talk radio is done via live remotes. These are remotes done from a stadium or a sponsor's business, but are necessary to the bottom line of the show (i.e. making money). A producer will sometimes work with a board op back in the studio who will ask as a call screener and will play sponsor ads during the breaks. The producer focuses on the people at the remote who they can place on the show for the talent to interview as well as become a gopher for the talent (getting drinks, etc).

Producing: Cell vs. Landline

Cell phones typically have less bars in less areas than they advertise. Cell phone callers also sound as if they are on permanent speaker phone. Whenever possible, especially with guests, have landline phones for interviews or callers. Cell phones sound like crap on radio, especially when a call is starting to drop and sounds garbled on the air.

Talent: Controversial Is Not Conversational

You can be the biggest talk of the town for about a month, calling out every person in the sports community. You can lead the band-wagon to getting a coach fired or a player benched. You can mean, nasty things and make everyone listen to you. And then, in about month two, you will be out of a job. Why? Because sports talk needs listeners and it needs guests. The audience also does not respect out-of-control people for long, especially when you end up raging on a favorite player or coach. People will put up with it for a while, but in the end, being controversial will not sell and you will be out of a job.

Talent: Callers

Insulting the callers is the first way to get yourself out of sports talk. Callers mean listeners, and the more listeners you angry, the less audience you end up having. Respect their opinion, hear it out, and argue with each caller effectively. Just because you have a forum to speak the loudest (sports talk), does not mean that you have the only true opinion. Speak in points that refer back to disagreement with the caller, but make sure that the caller understands that you respect their point of view too.

Example

Talent: Steve, welcome to sports radio 820.

Steve: Hi, Bill. I think that we should fire the coach because we 10-23 the season.

Talent: Well, it's the mid-point of the season, Steve.

Steve: But that doesn't make it alright. We've lost our last games by 20 points or more. Sometime has to change.

Talent: Look, Steve, I'm not defending the coach when I say this, but I do think that since we won the division last year, we should give him more of a chance. I thank you for the call though.

Notice that the Talent allowed Steve to make his point and did not insult the caller by telling him that he was an idiot or moron for wanting to fire the coach. Instead, the Talent pointed out what he thought were good reasons to keep the coach, thus keeping the argument civil and interesting. He also thanked the caller for calling in, thus retaining the caller as a listener even though the talent and caller disagreed on the subject. Neither side went away from the subject feeling that they were cut off or ignored or insulted. It also likely made one or two new people feel encouraged that they could call, argument a non-popular point with the talent and not feel that they are going to get bashed because of it.

Talent: Intro Segments

Each hour allows the talent to fully expand what is going on in the entire hour through an intro segment. The segment starts out as a rant on something, usually a game or issue that is facing sports, then teases the listeners with what is to come in the rest of the hour.

Example

"The Braves lost their twenty-third game last night, yet something we have come to expect from the clowns on the bay. I watched the television as horror as yet another game lost from a team that won the division last year. This is frightening. This not Braves basketball. Last time I checked, that guy coaching did not subscribe to this basketball either. What has happened? We'll discuss it with Jack Stone of the Times who covers the Braves and was there last night at the Forum to watch it. Also in this hour, expect Kristen Jones to stop by with a report on the NASCAR season, plus your phone calls…"

Talent: Guests

Every guest has something to sell. It may be a new season of their sport, a product that they are shilling, or an organization that they are a spokesperson for. Let them speak about. Remember that with guests, it is best to ask the question and be quiet. Let them fill the void and talk. The listeners want you to ask the questions, but they want to hear the guest, otherwise the show is just about you and nothing else. If that is the case, why have the producer schedule the guest in the first place? Ask power questions that turn guests into wisdom providers. It is also good to introduce the guest with a short recap of why the guest is important for the listeners to hear from. It also shows that the talent has some idea of who the guest is and their relevance to the program itself.

Chapter Eight
Show Prep For Sportscasting

It is everything that you should have in order to develop a good sportscast. Everyone who is successful on the air show preps as much as they can. Everyone who just "wings it" really keeps themselves from being successful.

Make a show prep binder

This is the best way to compile and keep your notes on everything that you need in order to have a successful sportscast. You should have the binder divided into several different parts. It would also be smart to have some pens, a yellow high lighter and a note pad handy, in case you need to be told something while on air.

Show Prep Binder Sections: **Pregame Intro – Game Highlights - Live Copy # 1 – Live Copy #2 – Live Copy #3 – Live Copy #4 – Live Copy #5 – Game Logs - Home Bios - Home Stats - Visitor Bios - Visitor Stats - Post Game/Misc.**

Pregame Intro: This is where your typed pregame intro goes. You should practice or go over it once or two prior to actually saying it on air. Separating this from the group of information you have in the show prep binder makes it easier to find when you are attempting to go LIVE with the broadcast.

Game Highlights: This is where you put down any possible highlights of interest that you need to mention during the game. These include 1,000 points for a career, rankings of a player in a conference, coaching records, etc. This will allow you to sound more knowledgeable about the game you are calling and enhance the broadcast.

Live copy 1-5: All of your live copy goes in this section. A good suggestion is to have the live copy in the order in which it appears. This will allow you to get to that section fast without missing a beat. Again, it is better to practice each live copy sheet prior to going live with the broadcast.

Game Logs: Placing all of your extra game log sheets in this section. You will take out what game logs you need prior to the broadcast and have it separate from the binder. Mainly this is a backup plan in case a game log goes missing or coffee/juice/water drenches your game log. No advertiser likes a game log which is coffee stained.

Home/Visitor Bios: This is where you should have a biography on each player and coach. Not just the stats, but the stupid stuff. If a player likes to sailing or another one is a water resource technician, this can separate your broadcast in those moments when the action is at a stand-still (namely free throws). *Example: "Steve Brown goes to the line for the 1-and-1, he's actually a pretty good quarters player. Apparently, no one his team can beat him because he just finds the glass. Brown hits the free throw on the front end of the 1-and-1, but no glass this time."*

Home/Visitor Stats: You should not only have current stats for the entire year, but also the last 3-4 game stat sheets that the home team has played. Use a yellow high lighter and seek out those interesting stats during the last few games. When you have a chance, utilize these as a mention. *Example: "Emily Brown has been perfect from 3-point tonight against Xaiver, she did the same thing two games ago against Marshall with an 11-for-11 performance behind the arc in the 102-92 victory December 13."*

Post Game/Misc: This is where you keep all of the extra stuff. In case you have a guest coming on, a special announcement (like the game next week will be on at 3 p.m. instead of 7 p.m.), etc.

Weekly Releases

Most colleges will have a sports information director (SID) assigned to handle publicity requests.

Sometimes, these are half pay positions in which a coach or administrative assistant moonlights in order to cover their other half pay position within the department.

A lot of SIDs do place several key information documents on their website, in order to help streamline the process.

One of the necessary documents they place online is the weekly release, which has just about everything a sportscaster could want.

A weekly release will include the last two stat sheets for each home game, home quotes and notes, and other bits of information.

A good rule of thought is to look on both the home and away websites, to see if both are writing a weekly release. Both of these documents together can make a great sportscast.

OMAHA FIREBALLS BASKETBALL

Omaha University Fireballs (13-2 overall, 2-1 in conference)
Weekly Notes - Jan. 3, 2009
Upcoming: Jan. 6 vs. No. 3 Stevens Quarry State (11-4, 1-1)
Jan. 8 vs. No. 2 Missouri Valley College (15-0, 4-0)

Fireballs hits five 3-point shots to get overtime against Mississippi College, but lose in a heartbreaker

Gene Ain't Happy With Second Place: Head Coach Gene Upwright said that the Fireballs would not accept the second place trophy at the Sydney Tournament, after Fireballs drop a 123-120 overtime loss to Mississippi College in the tournament final Dec. 31, 2008. *"It just ain't us to finish second and I don't expect our players to be comfortable with it either."*

Other Quotes from Sydney Tournament:

"We go home with a championship or we don't eat during the night

2008-09 Men's Basketball Schedule		
Date	Opponent	Result
Nov. 3	#Pacific University	W, 91-49
Nov. 9	at $$$Washington State	L, 41-68
Nov. 12	at New Mexico	L, 57-92
Nov. 15	UC-Riverside	W, 59-51
Nov. 18	at $$Washington	L, 68-82
Nov. 21	vs. %Virginia Tech	L, 52-69
Nov. 23	vs. %Michigan	L, 53-61
Nov. 24	at %Alaska Anchorage	W, 64-62
Nov. 29	Santa Clara	L, 57-66
Dec. 3	at Missouri-Kansas City	W, 65-54
Dec. 5	at Kansas	L, 47-85
Dec. 9	at Idaho	L, 49-58
Dec. 14	Cascade	W, 91-59
Dec. 17	Portland	W, 84-75
Dec. 22	*Portland State	W, 58-57
Dec. 31	Mississippi College	L, 123-120
Jan. 3	*Stevens Quarry St	7 p.m.
Jan. 6	*Missouri Valley College	5 p.m.

Chapter Nine
Developing Your Writing Skills

Despite whatever your uncle, grandfather, father or friend thinks of sportscasting, it is not a business for the illiterate.

Frankly, if you do not develop exceptional writing skills, you will fail at sportscasting.

While some may believe this is hard to comprehend in an industry built on verbal communication, what you need to realize is that most of the verbal communication was written first, then it is delivered orally.

Those who are successful in broadcasting know how to write. In fact, they have developed writing skills which are comparable to most journalists. Period, end of sentence.

Writing takes time.

You have to focus each sentence, understand how to develop it into an orally satisfying manner, and retain the interest of your listening audience.

This starts with the opening script of your pregame show, which can make or break your broadcast.

Imagine your listening audience tuning into your broadcast, only to find the PBP stumbling around with their words and unable to really tell anyone why they should listen.

That is why writing is important. It lays the foundation for the rest of the broadcast and helps you succeed.

Writing The Pregame Intro

The Who, What, When, Where & How of journalism applied to the opening script of your basketball pregame show. General information is brought as a teaser in order to develop why your target audience should listen.

This develops further with more information which expands the reasoning behind why this game is important, what is going on, when it will happen, the location of the game and how it will be carried out. This is a general teaser with entices the listener with the sharpest of aspects.

A good rule of thought is that you pretend you are running up to a single person and telling them what is happened. Generally, in that type of information, you would cut to the chase and tell them exactly what they need to know immediately, then expand further later. This intro portion of the pregame script is no different.

```
INTRO
     Tonight the Simmons Bearcats boys basketball squad
looks to build on the momentum of their last win
against Wilson Devil Dogs.
     The Bearcats bring a 11-10 record into tonight's
road match up and will look to climb their way back
toward the top of the Metro League against the
OnAlaska Wildcats.
     The Wildcats enter tonight's contest having lost
7 of their last 8 with a 10-7 record on the year and
a 2-7 record in the conference. The Bearcats will be
led tonight by Junior Orville Carlson and Senior John
Rider.
     Long and Rider are coming off the last game which
saw them score in double figures and will look to
repeat that performance again tonight.
     On the other side of the ball, the Wildcats will be
led by Ernie Waywright. The Sophomore Forward led the
Wildcats in scoring in their last game here on their
home court against Centralia Cyclones.
     All will square off tonight; LIVE in Metro League
boy's basketball action here on the Bearcats Network,
coming up next...
```

Writing The Pregame Open

Now you have an expanded version of the intro, which showcases far more than just a teaser. This larger edition has been made in order to take those listeners who have already been snared by your daring teaser and holds onto them with more information. This pregame open explains in-depth why they should continue listening, raises the stakes higher as to what teams are playing and how this game fits into the overall arch of the season. This entire pregame open fits the pattern of Arch Story Structure.

OPENING

Hello fans and welcome to the Mead Bearcats pre-game show on the Bearcats Network here at KWKY. We're glad you could join us. I'm John Doe. Tonight we come to you live from OnAlaska, Ohio where we are in a Metro League matchup between the Bearcats and Wildcats.

One year ago, Orville Carlson was sitting on the Bearcats bench with a broken leg and watched his team go down in flames against the OnAlaska Wildcats in a shootout. Back after an intense rehab throughout the summer, Orville is now atop the Metro League leaders with 20.5 points and 10.6 rebounds per game and 19 Division I offers on the table. Across the floor, he faces a McDonald's All-American candidate in OnAlaska's Ernie Waywright, who has average 35 points and 20 rebounds per contest with a 6-8 frame.

In order to stop Waywright, Bearcats coach Hans Kilk, Jr. will be will be looking for numerous players to step into roles and make things happen. The bench has depth and over the past few games has seen plenty of action. Jack Black will be looked upon to provide some defense as he has come away with 62 steals on the season. Sam Sneed will need to help knock down some three-pointers as they have in the last two games. There are plenty of players that can help and with the improved defensive play of the team they just need to overcome the slow starts. If they can jump on this Wildcat team early they should be able to keep some distance with their persistent defense.

We'll come back with coach Kilk's thoughts after this on the Bearcats Radio Network... (**cue sponsors, then canned coaches corner**).

Arch Story Structure

Arch Story Structure has been around since people first started telling stories and is used in most percent of all of the world's stories, including radio and film. Sportscasting typically uses Arch Story Structure in order to develop its storyline.

Simply put, it is a format of beginning, middle, and end. Part of Arch Structure is an active protagonist who must struggle against increased antagonism into order to reach an ultimate and irreversible end.

Using Arch Story Structure, look again at the same open and see how it is used to develop the storyline of the game.

Notice that we are set up with a tragedy beyond the initial story of Simmon's Orville Carlson, who is returning from an injury the previous season and is now facing a league rival. Carlson was unable to help his team last season and it resulted in the loss.

This is the first amount of antagonism presented in the storyline to the listeners (will he or won't he return to form). Now, notice the second form of antagonism, a brief description of Carlson returning to form after a summer of rehab.

The third and ultimate form of antagonism which stands between Carlson and his goals comes in the form of Ernie Waywright, who seems to dominate the Metro League with his statistics and sheer size.

This sets a David vs. Goliath story, transforming a game between two schools into an ultimate showdown of essentially two characters who are fighting against each other to win. By focusing the storyline down to two characters, it intensifies the need to pay attention for the listeners.

Writing LIVE copy

Writing LIVE copy is important. There may be events that occur in which you need to make an announcement that is important to the listener, or it may be a way to sell additional sponsorship.

Thirty seconds of verbal wordage equals about five to six lines of text.

"THAT FAST BREAK IS BROUGHT TO YOU BY JOHN'S RC STORE IN SAMUEL'S PLACE. JOHN'S RC HAS FIFTY DIFFERENT RC CARS TO CHOOSE FROM, SO STOP BY FOR ALL OF YOUR ENTERTAINMENT NEEDS. REMEMBER, THINGS AT JOHN'S RC ARE GOING FAST."

Keep everything concise. Simplify the words in order to make sure that they are understood. You might need to practice a few times as well in order to ensure that you give a high quality read when you go LIVE with the copy. Writing in CAPS tends to also simplify the process as well.

Notice that writing LIVE copy is simplistic, but gives every detail of information possible.

John's RC is at Samuel's place, it has over 50 different cars, but none of that is important. How exactly you get there, from the start of the break, is important.

Notice that it is a FASTBREAK timeout that you are going into. The word "Fast" is used twice in order to convey a relation between why the timeout was taken and what the message is to the listener.

Keep this in mind as you begin to secure sponsorship. How you use their message may be the difference between a klunky break and a good spot.

Writing A Highlight Package

When writing a highlight package it is important to marry each of the images properly with the narration involved. Notice that each image focuses on a back and forth battle between Jefferies and Steves, likely set up by a LIVE introduction by the host who sets the table between the two.

The culmination is to show how close Jefferies came to success but failed, then transitions to an interview with Jefferies about the game.

VIDEO	AUDIO
CLIP: Jefferies slam Dunk (0:05)	NARRATOR Stan Jefferies shows his stuff with a jam to lead off the game.
CLIP: Steves Pass to Baxter, Alley-Op (0:05)	NARRATOR Steves answers later in the second with an alley-op to Baxter for 2.
CLIP: End of Game 3-pt Shot that misses (0:10)	NARRATOR It comes down to Jefferies, 2 seconds left, misses the 3 to lose it.

CLIP W/ AUDIO:
Jefferies talks about losing the game on the desperation 3 in the locker room (0:15).

Developing A Good Flow System

This chart may help you in developing a good flow system. It is designed to mirror that of football depth charts, in order for PBP announcers to find names quickly without having to look up little pencil written names in a book during the game. It may be useful to you in terms of PBP for basketball as well, as sometimes the names can be tricky and those few seconds that you can't come up with a name on-air, you can look down and find it easy enough with this chart.

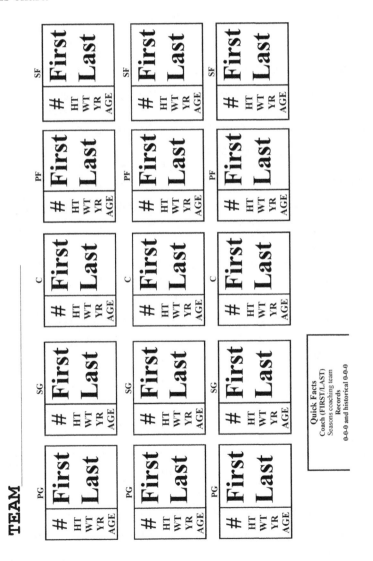

Chapter Ten
Developing A Sportscast Territory

Assuming that you can walk in and perform sportscasting without doing any leg work is rather naïve. Sure, you may have a radio station that wants to hire you, a sponsorship deal which rivals the NBA, but don't expect that your venue will be taken care of. People need to know who you are, what you are doing, and above all, go through the approval stages. This is especially true of high schools and colleges, where people cannot simply want onto campus and do whatever they wish.

Credibility – If you have contacts within a high school or college, it goes a long way toward getting your foot in the door. Several times, the first question posed to you will be "why do you want to do this for us?" If you reply that "its for the money," you won't see the pavement as it hits you. The last thing you want to do is find a school which already has a broadcaster. Typically, that broadcaster's credibility has been built through years of operation with the school and you shouldn't expect that you can just walk through the door, say "I've arrived" and have everything fall into place. Credibility takes work, it takes contacts, and above all, it takes decency.

Dress Attire – Anyone you meet connected with the school needs to respect you. The first way to do this is to show up in business attire. Regardless of how you feel about it, the school needs to determine your credibility. You must play the part if you are going to act in the play. Looking like a slob or someone who doesn't care will have people shrug you off or not return anymore phone calls.

Who To Contact First – When getting your foot in the door, don't wedge it in the wrong doorway, otherwise it may cut off your foot and leave you out in the cold. If you are attempting to broadcast for a high school or college, set up a meeting with the athletic director. Don't involve the basketball coach at this point. Instead, find out what the athletic director wants or thinks. They are the decision maker, not the coach (although a coach may believe otherwise).

The same is true for minor league teams. There are several in which the owner is the general manager and coach, so it various. However, attempting to contact anyone but the top person will likely get you no where. Sports information directors (SIDs) are also a key source to finding the right door to knock on at a college athletic department. You can look up who the sports information director is for a college in your town on the school's athletic website.

Be careful with SIDs though. A lot of them are typically interested in doing only Live Stats as a service for their parents & fans and not sportscasting. Live Stats is a program accessible through websites which shows the statistics as they happen with a 3-5 second delay. While some might find it interesting, most find it extremely boring.

Plan Out What You Are Providing – Are you buying time? Do you have a radio station willing to hire you and provide time for the game? Are you providing web streaming? Are you going to travel to each game or only do home games? You should know these things, any costs which are associated with them, and how you intend to have these services paid for.

Travel Concerns – Smaller colleges and some universities cannot afford to pay for travel expenses of sportscasters. Therefore, this may limit your involvement with that type of school unless you have funding via a radio station or sponsorship, etc. Assuming that you are traveling with the team, without making arrangements for funding or reimbursement, can get you in a ton of hot water.

Sponsorship Concerns – Some colleges and universities may want your product, however, they may not want to align themselves with specific sponsors. In this case, have a set form of guidelines in order to show how you will attain sponsorships etc. For instance, do not expect most schools to align themselves with adult stores, casinos, hard liquor ads or credit card companies. Most schools consider these to be the antithesis of their institution's mission. Be aware of what the school's mission is and be ready to align yourself with it, since you are hoping that the school will align itself with you.

For most minor league teams, that type of stuff goes out the window. Minor league teams may ask for a cut of your sponsorship deal as a matter of a rights fee. Sorry, but you are using their product to sell something. There is a give and a take with everything. However, if you are paying a rights fee, they should be paying for travel to and from their away games.

When to Approach - The best time to approach is 1-2 months after the last season culminated, not 1-2 weeks prior to the season starting. If you wait until the last minute, it is a scramble and likely you will not be the sportscaster for that team. Also, it gives everyone time to digest your proposal, what you intend to do for them, and how you will be compensated.

When Approaching Radio Stations – If you would like to cut to the chase and simply sportscast whatever basketball games a radio station provides, there are two ways to do it. First is to build yourself a killer aircheck. Second, is to hand-deliver a copy of the aircheck and your resume to the radio station's program director.

Making A Killer Resume – Highlight your skills as a sales person. Program directors are busy or just like to act busy. However, if you approach them with the mindset that you will help them *sell* something, program directors will listen. Program directors are usually fired based on sales at smaller stations, therefore anything that you can help a program director sell is worth about 10 points of interest on your side. People in radio make room for sales people. Air talent is a dime a dozen.

Commercial Call Letters On A Resume - A person with commercial call letters (example: KWUI 94.5 FM) looks great on a resume. Even if you have to work part-time as an announcer, these commercial caller letters get your foot in the door and on your way to a sportscasting career. If you don't have commercial call letters, as long as you have been calling games for a while, there is still hope to get a job, it just way take you promising to *sell* for the station.

Territory – Don't walk in on someone else's turf and expect to be welcomed with open arms. It can also happen later down the road to you. It is also unprofessional to sell a product, say a boy's high school basketball game, if the school hasn't authorized you to do so in advance. You can't just show up and expect to call a game, you should make all of the right contacts first, ensure that there is no one else you will be infringing on (another sportscaster who has been calling that team's games for 20 years). The general rule is that you respect others, they will respect you.

Planning Ahead – You should always plan a broadcast ahead. This means calling the school where you will be sportscasting that they have internet or phone line, a proper power supply, and to ensure that any other issues can be resolved. You do not want to attempt to resolve these issues at game time. Also, you shouldn't rely on a part-time school staff member at your high school to give you all of the proper details on internet or phone line access.

Making A Killer Aircheck

Although airchecks for sportscasting are a bit tough, if you fashion your aircheck correctly, you will have success.

Step One - Put about 2 minutes of opening highlights which set up entire plays (don't just include the dunks, but about three plays which set up the action with a culminating finish). Don't put music or anything underneath of the clips because it distracts from what the program director wants to listen to anyway.

Step Two - Place a quarter or half of one basketball game, unedited and continuous, in order to showcase your ability to keep up the action, present a mental picture for the audience through your verbal cues, etc. You had better not be screaming your way through, using a ton of crap lingo and catch phrases. This is where you establish your ability as a sportscaster, not where you make an ESPN highlight.

Step Three - Provide a pregame show to one of your broadcasts (minus the advertisements) which sets up your interviews skills and your intro/opening script.

What you should expect from the school or team:

Access

(interviews, stats, etc will be provided to you).

Professionalism

(space at the game table, etc).

Potential Sponsorship Opportunities

(if they have any sponsorship opportunities available for your broadcast, that they will likely give you the contact information to follow up with that potential sponsor).

What the school or team should expect from you:

Access

(broadcast, fairness, & little controversy).

Professionalism

(treating their players and coaches with respect, especially if they are younger).

Chapter Eleven
Selling Sponsorships

Selling sponsorship can be a pain in the butt. Especially if you try to prove everyone wrong by "going it alone" without any type of help. The first lesson of sales: People buy from their friends. This is the important rule of any sales. If you choose to sell sponsorships, which you may have to do either as an independent operator or as a member of a radio sportscast, there are quite a few things to remember.

Face it, sportscaster means sales: You are a salesperson. Forget the notion that you are the talent who can turn down the hard work of selling someone. That will not happen and if it does, everyone else in the world would be surprised. You are in sales. This is the business. Either learn to love it or leave it. No one will do the job for you. This is something you have to do in order to succeed.

Set a sponsorship cycle and stick to it: You should buy a calendar and have a sponsorship selling cycle of at least 200 days prior to your first game. This will allow you enough time to deal with all of the little things that will pop up (indecision, family issues, sponsorship follow-ups, new sales calls and new prospect leads).

Business Cards: You should have business cards with all of your contact information. Make your card memorable. Find a way for people to keep it and pass it along. Get business cards from everyone you meet and keep an organized list of your contacts (when you met them, where). Then try to set appointments or do follow-up. This is the best way to ensure a quality sale of your sportscast to the general businesses in the area.

Tax ID and Business License: If you are going to be in business for yourself, the government wants a piece of it. Usually, the fee is about $50 for a home-based business and about $20 plus paperwork for the state tax ID. This will also help you legitimize your sportscasting business, as well as give you the opportunity to gain access to various financial help, including business contacts who may end up advertising with you.

The business of sportscasting is fun to talk about: Face it, if you approach someone and tell them that you are in sportscasting, there is at least a mild interest in what you do. Its not like insurance or something boring. Working with sports is one of the best foots in the door you can have. Just about everyone either knows or thinks they know something about sports, and the majority love to talk about it. This is your best way to communicate that you have sponsorship available. Some of the people you speak with will not personally be those who buy sponsorship from you, however, they likely know people who will.

The secret of selling is who says what: If you say something good about yourself to a client, it sounds like your ego talking. If someone else says it about you to a client, it is money. Part of the secret of selling is to get referrals, which sure as hell beat up on cold calling someone, who likely does not want to buy from someone they do not know or trust.

Be prepared, look professional, and on time: This is a straight-laced business mentality. People judge on looks. They do not care that you like a pony tail or enjoy wearing stained sweat pants. You are trying to get them to part with their money. Your looks depend on their trust. If you decide to not show up to a meeting, it will get around. If you intend to "wing it" then expect to go home without a sale. Sponsorship sales are hard work. Mostly, they come directly from how you approach it.

Be good on the phone: You are in the verbal communication business. If you do not "give good phone" then you had better work on it or get out of sportscasting altogether. You need to be able to communicate with people. This means mumbling needs to be stop. This means you need to be able to be concise and direct about what you want. Remember, sponsors are busy too.

Set at least 10 appointments each week on Thursday and Friday: The front end of your week should be going to appointments for sponsorships. Typically, a Monday through Wednesday schedule is going to get you closer to talking with the decision makers. Use Thursday and Friday to call the sponsors to make appointments or do follow ups from previous appointments. This is a job at this point. Ensure that you have a one to two hour window in between each sales call, mainly because you do not want to be late for another appointment while your first appointment decide to have you reintroduce it to yet another partner.

Find a Decision-Maker: Everyone else is someone who cannot make a decision without someone else approving it. Usually they will road block without you getting anywhere. Ask who handles broadcasting sponsorship for the business. If you happen to get a secretary who is road blocking your inquiry, ask her if she can help you. When you find the person in charge of sponsorship, feel them out by setting an appointment. If, at the appointment, the person seems as if they are not a decision maker, help them progress the process into the next step. Ask if you need to attend any meetings with their bosses in order to help explain what you are providing. Be helpful, not pushy.

People buy from their friends: Learn to network, make friends, and have them reference you. Talk to the people who will benefit from your sportscast being on the air. Parents of players, boosters, local fans, etc. are a good way to start. Usually, they know the people you are trying to speak with. The difference is, with a friend recommending you, those decision makers will provide you extra time in sponsorship pitches. Commonly, people have already made up their mind to do *something* with you, it is just up to you to put their mind at ease.

The best inventory is limited: It does not matter if it is the first day of your sponsorship selling career, the best inventory you have is limited. While you should never openly lie about what you are selling and to whom, you should be willing to say that your best inventory is short supply. That you want to ensure that they are able to get the best sponsorship spots (usually at halftime or late in the second half of a basketball game), but that you have meetings scheduled with other sponsors who may want that portion of your inventory as well. If they ask who your sponsors are, have a good answer, have other sponsors scheduled that you are meeting with. Do not try to close them, simply let them know that while they have every opportunity to meet with you several times, the inventory you have today may not be the inventory you have tomorrow.

Always get the money up front and the contract is signed: Handshake deals always turn out bad. Get the sponsorship in writing via a contract. Pay a lawyer to draw a contract up, do not rely on a computer program to get to the details you need for the contract to binding.

Be Friendly With The Tire Kickers: Expect to have several hundred meetings with potential sponsors prior to going into the season. Expect more than a few to have several meetings with go nowhere. These prospects are called "Tire Kickers" and tend to feel people out. They are people who do not know you, are unsure of your product, and tend to want to keep knowing that you are serious about what you are doing.

Trade Does Not Pay the Bills: Do not take trade. It will not help you get an advertiser to pay money later on. It is better to not deal with someone who wants to give you trade, they tend to tell other potential sponsors about the fact that they had a deal in trade and all it does is reduce your product's value.

Rate Formula: Figure out the cost of time for each advertisement run divided by total ad time per hour, plus 100 percent. You have a finite inventory of good time slots.

Three different price points: People like deals. They also have different tastes. Some just want to dip their toe into the sponsorship, some want to have the maximum amount possible in order to blanket advertise. You need to have three different price points in order to help each sponsor find exactly the right fit for their dollar.

Setting Pricing: Set a maximum price, at least 150 percent higher than your lowest price and offer sponsorship spots on your broadcast for it. The middle price should be only about 75 percent higher than your lowest price, but do not give much more time than the lowest price offers. With the lowest price, offer a bargain basement price which is about 50 percent above your total costs to provide the sportscast. Also have a method of bumping smaller sponsorships for bigger ones. You want to sell as many medium sponsorships as possible.

Why Selling More Medium Sponsorships Is Good: You need your inventory filled. You need it filled prior to your first sportscast. It creates demand and allows you to tell your prospects that your current sponsorships are stacked and unless they intend to purchase a higher sponsorship than what you currently have, they will have to wait until next year. Prospects love to keep up with the Jones, especially if they are getting shut out of a good deal.

You need to do follow-up, don't expect a sale on the first call: Sales rarely happen on the first call. People need time to think, to ensure that they are making the right decision. Be patient.

Face-to-face is just as important: Meeting someone face to face is 10 times more effective than just a random call on the phone. Anyone can call on the phone. It means something when people meet someone and sell them through trust. It also allows people to have their questions answered and develop a good strategy for whether or not they should be sponsoring your sportscast.

Attend as many organized functions are you can: People love to talk sports, so you instantly have the best foot in the door possible. Attend every luncheon or function you can where you can meet people. Do not sit in the corner with your friends. Hand out as many business cards, exchange cards, and get to know the people who are around you. Know them, become their friend, and you will sell them quicker. Do not simply "sell" someone at these meetings. That rings false and is usually a way to lose a possible sale. There are several business to business meetings in every city, but no one wants to speak to an insurance salesman (usually reminds people of mortality), but sports is an instant connector. You can speak about the upcoming schedule, the current or past year, or the player or coach who is a genius for your team. Everything you say is more likely to sell if you keep it from being a blatant pitch. Let the part about your sponsorship, your huge listenership, etc. come naturally into the conversation. Do not force it.

Don't get lazy because of new technology: You need to pound the pavement. E-mails are useless and too easy to delete, especially if you send something unsolicited. You need to have a face to face, so the decision maker can trust you. It is the only way to sell. Don't be a spam king with your e-mail. It is usually annoying.

Retention is because of value received (it's a two-way street): If you sell a business a sponsorship, you need to make sure that they receive value in return. If that means you hand out extra flyers to fans at the venues you sportscast, or tell the entire football team to eat at that restaurant once a week, do it. Sponsorships mean that they are taking a chance on you. A lot of companies are not Pepsi or Walmart. These smaller companies need to track that their sponsorship with you is effective and brings people through the doors. They cannot afford blanket advertising. If a small business spends money with you, they need people coming through their doors because of it. No only can you harm a business owner by not giving them value, you also potentially cost other businesses from receiving sponsorship as well. That is not a good thing, since karma can be a killer.

If you attempt to "close" someone with a sponsorship, you tend to lose them: People are jaded and know when they are being closed on in a sales pitch. The limited time offer does not make anyone feel urgent about buying a sponsorship. In fact, it may be considered a turn-off. You should be willing to continue answering their questions, attempting to help them through the process.

Added Value Principle: The more added value, beyond what a sponsor had already expected to pay for, that the sponsor receives from you, the more likely they will return as a sponsor for the following broadcast or season. One way to do this as a sportscaster is to get a banner from the sponsor and have it placed up in the gym (with the permission of the team). Or hand out flyers, bumper stickers, etc., from that sponsor.

Listenership

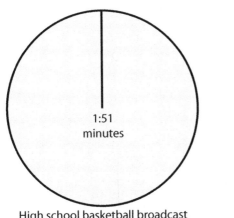

1:51
minutes

High school basketball broadcast
average listening time

31
minutes

Regular radio broadcast average
listening time

Any sponsor is going to attempt to find out what your listenership is for your broadcasts.

It is important to your sponsors that you are not merely broadcasting into the sea of white noise known as the internet or terrestrial radio.

That being said, it is a good idea to attempt to showcase how much time a person devotes to your sportscast as opposed to other broadcasts. A good way to illustrate this is through the average time concept.

What is the difference in average time a person in your area listens to any broadcast and the average time a person in your area listens to your sportscast.

If you also purchasing time from a local radio station, ask for a demographic of their listenership, etc.

Even if you are going independent online, still ask the radio station for their information, which is good research as you begin your endeavor into marketing.

Income of Listenership

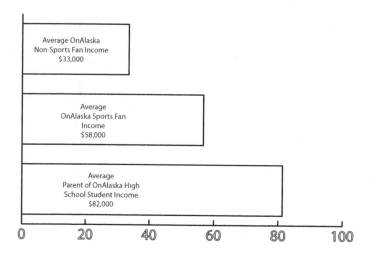

Think as your sponsor would think. Find the information you would want to know if you were considering sponsorship of an item. Remember, as a business owner, you would want to see people returning back through your doors if you sponsored a sportscast. Nothing is done for charity and your investment in any advertisement would need to show a return.

As a business owner, you would also want to ensure that you are targeting the right people with your sponsorship dollar. You may want females ages 34-54 or residents with an income higher than $45,000 per year. A car dealer does not want to target children ages 8-12 any more than toy store wants to target single males ages 25-38.

All of this depends on what your listenership is, who you believe as a sportscaster you are attempting to reach, and the businesses which would benefit from sponsoring your sportscast. Gaining sponsorship from a business which does not hit your target audience's interests does little good for anyone. Break down average times that your listeners ages and incomes for any potential sponsor to see. You can gather some of this information by looking online for county/city statistics on income, population, etc. All of this information should be close to accurate.

Comparison of Competition

Area Terrestrial & Internet Stations	Day signal Watts	Night signal Watts	Format
GAMERADIO.COM	200K Hits	506K Hits	SPORTS
WVI 520AM	5,000	5,000	Talk
WIRO 720AM	50,000	50,000	Talk
WTTH 790AM	50,000	5,000	Talk
WXXI 810AM	50,000	10,000	Talk
WJR 960AM	50,000	50,000	Sports
WAXWORKS.COM	50K Hits	100K Hits	Talk
JAMALRADIO.COM	67K Hits	25K Hits	Talk
WOLFHSRADIO.COM	5K Hits	14K Hits	Sports
WITZ 1420AM	1,000	890	Talk

Sponsors also want to know what the reach of your sportscasts will be compared to other stations (internet or terrestrial) in the area. While you should never provide false information in terms of raw numbers, you should provide local stations which place your sportscast into the best light.

A 100,000 watt power pig AM station is going to trounce you in ratings regardless. So why place something like that on your comparison list? That would be like comparing an NFL linebacker to a high school linebacker. There is too great of a difference to determine a good comparison between the two. Therefore, the comparison should be with "like stations" which exist and charge close to what you charge.

With the comparison of "like stations" on your list, you can isolate and illustrate how your product stands up with other products in the local area. It will also justify pricing of sponsorship as well as why a sponsor should consider you over the competition.

Price Levels & Value of Sponsorship

	Triple Double	6th Man	Slam Dunk	Three Pointer
Price Level	$5,000	$2,500	$1,500	$1,000
1 Headline sponsorship of "Coaches Show"	X			
1 Headline sponsorship of "Pregame show"	X	X		
1 Headline sponsorship of "Postgame show"	X	X		
Two :30 second ads				X
Five :30 second ads		X	X	
Eight :30 second ads	X			
1 GAMERADIO.com button (Oct. 07-June 07)	X	X	X	
Sponsorship of online e-mails	X	X	X	X
Signage in gym	X	X	X	X
Sponsorship of 1 Player of the Game	X	X	X	X

Spots available	1 min	30 sec
Coaches Show	3	3
Pregame	2	3
Game Action	2	17
Postgame	2	3

Notice that this quad-level pricing is already deceptive compared to the rules that were set up earlier in this chapter. Why? Because the top level of $5,000 is actually an all-in price, made to show the top level sponsorship of the broadcast. It will likely never be purchased, but ends debate as far as how high a sponsor can go to "own" the broadcast.

The real pricing is $2,500 to $1,500 to $1,000. This structure is set up to allow the sponsor to feel as if they can reach the secondary top level ($2,500) without it being the highest paid for the broadcast. Many sponsors will go for the top level rather than the mid or lowest level, simply because they will be enticed by the possibility of becoming the secondary top sponsor without spending the top price.

Chapter Twelve
Broadcast Equipment

The following equipment is useful for most sportscasters. It depends on what you have and what you want to do. Also included are two audio stream providers. All of the equipment suggestions are ones which have been widely used over the last few years, however, this book is merely pointing you in the general direction of what you need and not an endorsement of any product.

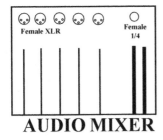

Laptop
Cost - $800

This laptop should pack enough of a punch at an affordable price. It also needs to have enough USB ports, mic and headset inputs and ability to be flexible for audio streaming & editing.

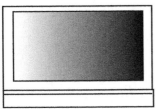

Sound Mixer
Cost - $1000

This is a more professional mixer which allows the user to carry up to 8 inputs, four from XLR males. This works well especially for judging voice levels during games, etc.

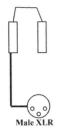

Headset with Microphone
Cost - $300

This headset provides good quality and allows the user to manipulate the bendable microphone front. The sound quality in the headphones also works well when having to listen for cues from back in studio.

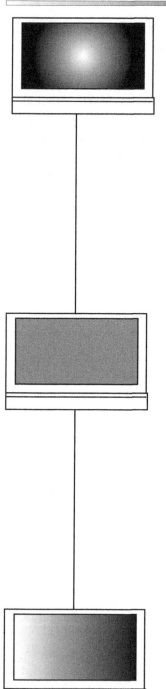

Audacity Editing Software
Cost - Free

This is an excellent audio editing software tool which allows you to create canned audio, along with bed insertion, for great sponsor ads.

Windows Media Encoder 9
Cost - Free

You need this in order to encode audio/ video streaming to a service provider. It is free and can also record your stream for playback later.

WinAmp
Cost - Free

This program is great for building various playlists to establish your breaks for pregame, timeouts, halftime, etc. Very flexible and easy to use.

Equipment Hookup

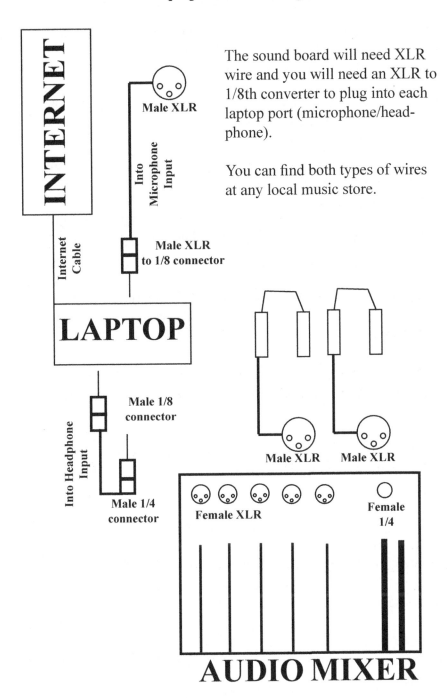

The sound board will need XLR wire and you will need an XLR to 1/8th converter to plug into each laptop port (microphone/headphone).

You can find both types of wires at any local music store.

Push-Pull for Internet Streaming

There are two methods of streaming your information through an encoder, the push method or the pull method.

PUSH – You are sending the signal out to a webstream site which will receive it and stream whatever it is given.

The push method is generally used for non-video webstreaming, due to it being unreliable.

With audio streaming being at a lower band of data consistently (up to 134kbps), the push method is reliable enough to maintain the stream connection.

When pushing something, the receiver does not notice if there are any signal disruptions or breaks, therefore the push signal can get lost at anytime.

The push method is good for navigating through firewalls especially on college campuses, which may not allow for the pull method.

A push method is one which will continue to generate data without external prompting until told to stop.

PULL – Your laptop acts as the receiver, with the webstream site grabbing the huge chunks of data from the laptop through the stream. A pull method will generate one chunk of data at a time in response to an explicit request for more data.

This is generally the best way to initiate videostreaming because of the large data chunks which need to be sent through the internet portal.

Chapter Thirteen
Developing A Commercial Log System

If you refuse to read this section or develop a commercial log, you will likely fail at sportscasting. The commercial log system does not have to match the ones found in this notebook, forever, they should at least be treated as a good starting point for those wish to present a professional broadcasts.

The commercial log system is not just for commercials, its also to protect your voice and keep you from talking for the entire two hours of the game.

Commercial logs were developed as a way to help the advertiser confirm that their sponsorship spots were being run and at what time.

The system, if not used, will force your broadcast to sound unprofessional and haphazard. Thus, do not expect a ton of sponsorship if you refuse to confirm that the spots ran and at what time during the game.

It comes with the territory as a sportscaster that you develop a commercial game log system, then send copies back to the station or mail them out to your sponsors.

This is a way to confirm to sponsors that you indeed ran their advertisements, that you were honest and attempted like hell to get every sponsor's advertisement in on time, etc.

Newspapers perform a similar method with a practice called "tear sheets" in which they mail directly to their sponsors the newspaper advertisements which were run.

So if you were hesitating on developing a commercial log system, think again. Everyone does it for a specific reason. The reason is getting paid.

Pregame Commercial Log

The pregame log really sets up your broadcast from the start. Notice that in this log for the pregame, you have exactly 12 sponsorship spots to fill as well as run. Three of those spots are also :60 seconds.

This also helps guide you in a format with the pregame show in general, so that things are presented evenly without any opportunity to get out of hand. It gives you structure as to when the lineups need to be return, when the taped interview with the coach and player are going to be broadcast, and which sponsors are run at which times. As stated earlier in Chapter Ten, sponsors like to be married around certain events or levels when they believe that listeners will be paying attention the most.

This pregame schedule is set for 15 minutes prior to tip-off. Unless you are a professional organization with a large listenership, as well as have the opportunity for multiple guests and call-in listeners, it is best to stay within a 15 minute start-up window. Otherwise, things get out of hand quick and you end up with bad or dead air.

Men's Basketball Game Commercial Log
Date_____   Opponent _____
I hereby certify that the commercials listed aired at the times
listed (name of announcer)_____ Date _____

Segment	Break #	Spot Title	Length	Client	Time Aired	Initial
Pregame	LIVE	Pregame Intro	:20	LIVE	_____	____
Pregame	#1	Station ID	:10	Inhouse	_____	____
Pregame	#1	**SPONSOR**	:30	AD	_____	____
Pregame	LIVE	Lineup/Matchup	2:00	LIVE	_____	____
Pregame	#2	**SPONSOR**	:30	AD	_____	____
Pregame	#2	**SPONSOR**	:60	AD	_____	____
Pregame	TAPE	Coaches Corner	2:00	Inhouse	_____	____
Pregame	#3	**SPONSOR**	:30	AD	_____	____
Pregame	#3	**SPONSOR**	:30	AD	_____	____
Pregame	#3	**SPONSOR**	:30	AD	_____	____
Pregame	#3	**SPONSOR**	:30	AD	_____	____
Pregame	TAPE	Player Interview	2:00	Inhouse	_____	____
Pregame	#4	**SPONSOR**	:60	AD	_____	____
Pregame	#4	**SPONSOR**	:30	AD	_____	____
Pregame	LIVE	Wrapup Pre	2:00	LIVE	_____	____
Pregame	#5	**SPONSOR**	:60	AD	_____	____
Pregame	#5	**SPONSOR**	:30	AD	_____	____
Pregame	#5	**SPONSOR**	:30	AD	_____	____
Pregame	TAPE	Pregame Out	:20	Inhouse	_____	____
Pregame	#5	Station ID	:10	Inhouse	_____	____

1st/2nd Half Commercial Log

Because both the first half and the second half are similar in how the commercial logs are developed, they were included on one page instead of two. Both sets have varying times of :30 and :60 commercial spots. Generally, each timeout and break is worth about :60 seconds. Going beyond that in the game can force you to either cut the commercial short (which is not good if the sponsor listens or hears about it from someone else) or miss some of the game trying to fulfill the spot.

Basketball Game Commercial Log
Date_____   Opponent _____
I hereby certify that the commercials listed aired at the times
listed (name of announcer)_____ Date _____

Segment	Break #	Spot Title	Length	Client	Time Aired	Initial
1st Half	#1	SPONSOR	:60	AD	_____	_____
1st Half	#2	SPONSOR	:30	AD	_____	_____
1st Half	#2	SPONSOR	:30	AD	_____	_____
1st Half	#3	SPONSOR	:30	AD	_____	_____
1st Half	#3	SPONSOR	:30	AD	_____	_____
1st Half	#4	SPONSOR	:60	AD	_____	_____
1st Half	#5	SPONSOR	:30	AD	_____	_____
1st Half	#5	SPONSOR	:30	AD	_____	_____
1st Half	#6	SPONSOR	:30	AD	_____	_____
1st Half	#6	SPONSOR	:30	AD	_____	_____
1st Half	#7	SPONSOR	:30	AD	_____	_____
1st Half	#7	SPONSOR	:30	AD	_____	_____
1st Half	#8	SPONSOR	:60	AD	_____	_____
1st Half	#9	SPONSOR	:60	AD	_____	_____
1st Half	#10	SPONSOR	:30	AD	_____	_____
1st Half	#10	SPONSOR	:30	AD	_____	_____

Basketball Game Commercial Log
Date_____   Opponent _____
I hereby certify that the commercials listed aired at the times
listed (name of announcer)_____ Date _____

Segment	Break #	Spot Title	Length	Client	Time Aired	Initial
2nd Half	#1	SPONSOR	:60	AD	_____	_____
2nd Half	#2	SPONSOR	:30	AD	_____	_____
2nd Half	#2	SPONSOR	:30	AD	_____	_____
2nd Half	#3	SPONSOR	:30	AD	_____	_____
2nd Half	#3	SPONSOR	:30	AD	_____	_____
2nd Half	#4	SPONSOR	:60	AD	_____	_____
2nd Half	#5	SPONSOR	:30	AD	_____	_____
2nd Half	#5	SPONSOR	:30	AD	_____	_____
2nd Half	#6	SPONSOR	:30	AD	_____	_____
2nd Half	#6	SPONSOR	:30	AD	_____	_____
2nd Half	#7	SPONSOR	:30	AD	_____	_____
2nd Half	#7	SPONSOR	:30	AD	_____	_____
2nd Half	#8	SPONSOR	:60	AD	_____	_____
2nd Half	#9	SPONSOR	:60	AD	_____	_____
2nd Half	#10	SPONSOR	:30	AD	_____	_____
2nd Half	#10	SPONSOR	:30	AD	_____	_____

Halftime Commercial Log

Halftime is where your feet get put to the fire. If you cease to have a good show and the game appears to be lop-sided, you will drop listeners quickly.

This is not good for the broadcast, for retention of sponsors, and for your future endeavors as a sportscaster. The best way to prevent all of those bad to worse scenarios from happening is to develop a good halftime commercial game log.

Notice that the stats and synopsis of the first half are presented first. This is to help listeners grasp what details have happened in the game and how the game has developed.

This is especially true if you are broadcasting an event where there is a record or some important information happening in the game.

This mission with the halftime show is to blend the LIVE broadcast with taped interviews. If you can get a LIVE interview, that is great, however, that likely will not happen as often as you would like or hope.

Basketball Game Commercial Log
Date_____   Opponent _____
I hereby certify that the commercials listed aired at the times
listed (name of announcer)_____ Date _____

Segment	Break #	Spot Title	Length	Client	Time Aired	Initial
Halftime	LIVE	Halftime Intro	:20	LIVE	_____	____
Halftime	#1	Station ID	:10	Inhouse	_____	____
Halftime	#1	**SPONSOR**	:30	**AD**	_____	____
Halftime	LIVE	Stats/Synopsis	2:00	LIVE	_____	____
Halftime	#2	**SPONSOR**	:30	**AD**	_____	____
Halftime	#2	**SPONSOR**	:60	**AD**	_____	____
Halftime	TAPE	Athlete of Week	2:00	Inhouse	_____	____
Halftime	#3	**SPONSOR**	:30	**AD**	_____	____
Halftime	#3	**SPONSOR**	:30	**AD**	_____	____
Halftime	#3	**SPONSOR**	:30	**AD**	_____	____
Halftime	#3	**SPONSOR**	:30	**AD**	_____	____
Halftime	TAPE	Interview	2:00	Inhouse	_____	____
Halftime	#4	**SPONSOR**	:60	**AD**	_____	____
Halftime	#4	**SPONSOR**	:30	**AD**	_____	____
Halftime	LIVE	Wrapup Halftime	2:00	LIVE	_____	____
Halftime	#5	**SPONSOR**	:60	**AD**	_____	____
Halftime	#5	**SPONSOR**	:30	**AD**	_____	____
Halftime	#5	**SPONSOR**	:30	**AD**	_____	____
Halftime	TAPE	Halftime Out	:20	Inhouse	_____	____
Halftime	#5	Station ID	:10	Inhouse	_____	____

Postgame Commercial Log

The Post Game log is crucial. This is where your bread and butter as far as ad revenue really kicks in.

A sponsor wants to make sure that people are listening at this point, mainly because any spots you didn't get to comes into play. It is also a way to hit some extra spots on the back end of the broadcast and make a few extra dollars.

Hit the synopsis and recap part of the post game show first. Two reasons: 1. The coach may or may not be back from any other commitments they have after the game. 2. It allows the listener to recap exactly what happened and how it happened.

Then, get the coach and the player lined up. Make an assistant coach a "buddy" in order to grab the player and coach for you. Get them on their air, let them catch their breath, and always have a back up plan. Everyone wants to chat up your ear when they win, they tend to get quiet or "forget" that they had promised to go on the postgame show when they lose.

Basketball Game Commercial Log
Date_____   Opponent _____
I hereby certify that the commercials listed aired at the times
listed (name of announcer)_____ Date _____

Segment	Break #	Spot Title	Length	Client	Time Aired	Initial
Postgame	LIVE	Postgame Intro	:20	LIVE	_____	_____
Postgame	#1	Station ID	:10	Inhouse	_____	_____
Postgame	#1	**SPONSOR**	:30	**AD**	_____	_____
Postgame	LIVE	Synopsis/Recap	2:00	LIVE	_____	_____
Postgame	#2	**SPONSOR**	:30	**AD**	_____	_____
Postgame	#2	**SPONSOR**	:60	**AD**	_____	_____
Postgame	LIVE	Coach Interview	2:00	LIVE	_____	_____
Postgame	#3	**SPONSOR**	:30	**AD**	_____	_____
Postgame	#3	**SPONSOR**	:30	**AD**	_____	_____
Postgame	#3	**SPONSOR**	:30	**AD**	_____	_____
Postgame	#3	**SPONSOR**	:30	**AD**	_____	_____
Postgame	LIVE	Player Interview	2:00	LIVE	_____	_____
Postgame	#4	**SPONSOR**	:60	**AD**	_____	_____
Postgame	#4	**SPONSOR**	:30	**AD**	_____	_____
Postgame	LIVE	Wrapup Post	2:00	LIVE	_____	_____
Postgame	#5	**SPONSOR**	:60	**AD**	_____	_____
Postgame	#5	**SPONSOR**	:30	**AD**	_____	_____
Postgame	#5	**SPONSOR**	:30	**AD**	_____	_____
Postgame	TAPE	Postgame Out	:20	Inhouse	_____	_____
Postgame	#5	Station ID	:10	Inhouse	_____	_____

Chapter Fourteen
Final Thoughts

Below are some final thoughts that were random in nature, but probably needed to be addressed somewhere. Beyond those thoughts, on the final pages, are field/court marks and terms for anyone wishing to sportscast other events such as a volleyball, ice hockey, football, and baseball. With the help of several coaches, just about every term imaginable was written down and included.

Don't Just Shout

Dick Vitale is one thing, you are another, and Brian Bosworth is another. Vitale uses his voice to feed off the energy of the crowd, etc., but it does tend to be a television experience, not an audio one. Vitale also does stop screaming when the energy of the court takes over the energy of the crowd. Brian Bosworth, a former NFL player who served a color analyst for the defunct XFL, screamed every time he opened his mouth. Bosworth's stint with the XFL was termed as "white noise," distracting instead of enhancing the broadcast. Just a thought on different styles.

What Format of Broadcast to Use

Radio Stations typically have various phone receiver boxes which use a POTS line, the best phone line possible. However the receiver does work well with PBX lines. Some of this is greek to the sportscaster, but the radio engineer at the station should be able to answer any questions you have on this.

Direct Internet is preferred when going with an audio stream. Wireless Internet dims in and out, meaning your broadcast will sound the same to anyone at home listening. Cellular phone sportscasts sound like crap and should be avoided, especially because all it takes is a cloud in the sky for you to get one bar on your phone and the thing goes dead right as the team makes a come back.

Rundown Sheets

When dealing with a minor league team or college which has an SID, you will typically get a rundown sheet. Request your sheet via email about a day prior, in order to ensure that you are aware of any changes to it. The rundown sheet will detail when the coach or a player that you need to interview for the pregame show is available. It may also help you snag an opposing coach or player if you also want their inclusion into your show.

Voice Levels

If the needle or meter bounces in the red on your sound mixer while you talk, then falls back down, you are alright. If the needle or meter stays in the red and never falls back down, it means you need to lower the volume on your microphone. Otherwise it distorts the sound of your microphone and leaves your sportscast sounding like crap.

Court Microphone

Frankly, a microphone on the court does nothing to enhance the broadcast. Why? Because your headset will usually pick up enough sound off of the floor. Some sportscasters swear by them, use your discretion and try out a few different ways. One size does not fit all.

Media Timeouts

Some high school leagues have media timeouts, other leagues do not. The NCAA and NAIA both adhere to media timeouts and some junior colleges do as well. It all depends on where you are at. Make sure that you have the athletic director or sports information director alert the referees that you have a media broadcast and let them make the call. Media timeouts are a boon for sportscasts, so you should attempt to have them at every game, because you can sell sponsorships at those breaks too.

Sports Information Directors

SIDs are typically stat geeks who can write. Even they will tell you that and be proud of it. If you need help at the game table, SIDs are the ones who can provide it for you, especially if it is a rule or stats question. Most SIDs adhere to the rules and regulations of CoSIDA, their membership organization.

What that means to you is that most CoSIDA members, if not all, will provide you with one or two game table places (if you bring a stats person), a stats sheet printed out at every timeout, a link to Live Stats (if they have it), a media guide of their team, game notes detailing information about both teams as well as players & coaches before and after the game.

Don't assume anything, especially on the road. It is best to have your school's SID contact the opponent's SID, arrange all of the things you need (internet, phone line, game table space, etc.) prior to arriving. Nothing makes an SID more friendly than a person who shows up unannounced and thinks they run the show. In fact, SIDs will likely prove to you who runs the show at the game table.

Promote Your Broadcast

Regardless of which venue you have your audio broadcast on, you need to promote it. No one will know about it unless you tell them. So make sure that you do. Some ideas include having a friend hand out flyers about the audio broadcast at games, telling the PTA about the broadcasts in order to get them to listen, calling up the sports editor at the local newspaper to make sure that the broadcast is listed along with the game times. Promote, promote, promote. You are doing this not only for yourself but for your sponsors who have invested in you.

Extra Things to Bring

Include a long orange extension cord, a power strip, extra batteries for the laptop and sound mixer, and anything else you can think of. Every place is different and don't expect everyone to have everything, if you call up two days before and ask. Assume the worst and pray for the best.

On Their Time

When setting up interviews, remember that while time is money for you, the coaches and players also have other outside interests that absorb their time. That being said, don't get frustrated with lateness out of the coaches and players you are attempting to interview, they are doing you a favor. While this may be something you want to disagree with, until you let them in on your profit sharing, don't expect them to be totally eager to show up instantly upon command.

Different Voices

Newspaper don't refuse ink and radio loves different voices. When developing any type of commercials or intros to the pregame, game and postgame, use different voices to narrate. Find your spouse or a little kid (this actually works wonders because people like to listen to little kids). Different voices makes your broadcast sound more professional, as if you have a team of people surrounding you, and enlivens the broadcast fully.

LIVE Interviews

Have some questions ready and be prepared. This comes with advance knowledge of the subject or person you are speaking with. Treat the subject or the person as if they are very important and that you are privileged to have on. Both aspects will help the interview go well, and really, the person is helping generate listeners to you by creating an atmosphere as part of your broadcast. If you don't know anything about them and they are a last minute addition, ask some open ended questions to learn about them while on-air.

Versatility

Too often sportscasters attempt to call only one sport, such as football, mainly because they love that sport. A challenge to anyone is to call a sport you really can't stand. Try volleyball or tennis. Think about how hard something is to call when you don't really know what is going on. Now think of how the listener feels, when you don't properly describe something, even that sport you so love.

Buying Time

Local small market stations have a lot of time to fill, and in some cases, sell their times in one to two hour blocks to locals who then sell advertising and place their own broadcasting during those blocks on the small market station. Some sportscasters have become very successful by buying local time, selling corporate sponsorships, and then broadcasting the games. A word to the wise, however, you must insure what you are guaranteeing. Many of the small market stations want their cash up front, may not have the times available to air your games live, or may not have the interest. It takes a lot of work to buy time, then resell it, but there is also a lot of interest from local sponsors who can hear your game on the air anytime they want.

Being a salesperson

Face it. Regardless of why you want to be in sportscasting, you are a sales person. You need to sell every listener on why they should be listening. You need to keep them listening through the breaks in the action (NOTE: Corporate Sponsors need people to buy their products, they don't just pay big money for ad space as an act of charity). If you don't attempt to sell the product thoroughly, you aren't going to be success at it. Worst off, you will sound bad on the air.

Prepare, Prepare, Prepare

In further chapters, show prep will be discussed. Don't think you can just go on air and "wing it" if you want to be successful at sportscasting. Typically, it makes for bad broadcasting when people "wing it" because they think its too much work. What you put into something is what you get out of it. The harder you work, the better you sound. Just because you can fool your spouse, parents or friends by sounding like crap doesn't mean you're sounding "awesome" to everyone else. Basically, if you sound like crap and no one has the heart to tell you otherwise.

Criticism

Your parents, spouse, and friends are not going to be good critics of your broadcasting work. Find someone isn't into sports or has no interest in telling you that "you're the greatest broadcaster ever. EVER!" Find that type of person (usually your spouse's best friend who doesn't approve of you) and give them $20 to tell you everything that's wrong with the broadcast. Trust me, they will do it, and not for the $20. In fact, they will probably be so harsh that you will attempt to defend yourself. Just take the load of criticism and work from it. Honesty sucks, seriously, but it helps as much as it hurts.

Sportscasting Platforms

Congratulations. You are in the one business that is constantly gaining more opportunities, mainly due to the internet, XM radio, and the abundance of sports teams. The internet used to be a joke, something that people never understood to be a key part of how to broadcast audio. ITunes and Real Player changed that outlook and now it's respectable enough.

Negativity Toward Internet Broadcasts

For most independent operators, purchasing time on local radio stations is a way to negate the suggestion that the internet is a focused product and not made for "passive people." Basically that theory arrives at the thought that no one will pass a dial and stop accidentally finding the game on and stay tuned. With the internet, people have to select on the link in order to listen to it, thus they have to be "active" in their approach to the internet radio broadcast. However, the likelihood that "passive" listeners would stop on a station they had no reason to listen to prior, for a sportscast, can be marginal at best. With internet broadcasts, you can show "real" numbers where you can specifically detail the amount of people listening, the peak connections to your server at one time, and the listening time of each fan. This can also be huge for advertisers, who may not get real research from small market terrestrial radio stations. Both broadcasts have their detractors regardless of where you end up with your sportscast.

Things to Expect

Expect that you will be working long hours and have nothing to show for it but a tape and a couple of dollars missing from your wallet. Expect that your spouse or significant other will not understand why you do this. Expect to miss dinner or other appointments because you are working at a job that pays nothing. Expect to lose money if you attempt to buy time and sell the sponsorship itself if you don't take it seriously or start right before the season. Expect your boss at your real job not understanding why you do what you do. Expect people to suggest that you would be farther ahead (promotions, etc) if you didn't devote your time to sportscasting. Expect to live or die with the team you are sportscasting for, especially when it is a girl's/women's team and they lose (mainly because they are usually the nicest people and don't deserve to face such heartache, trust me, it'll kill you too). Expect to have a fulfilling time doing something that other people mock, highlight your errors and that your loved ones secretly or publicly wish you would quit. What you will experience is the goal of being passionate, something that people don't attempt to risk enough to feel anymore. You are one of the lucky ones... congrats.

Index

B
Baseball Layout, 41
Blue Language, 22

C
Cheat Sheet, 3
Color Analyst
    Amateur v Pro Rule, 55
    Blowouts, 55
    Calling out, 56
    Duties, 12
    Homer v Homespun, 56
    Injuries, 58
    Know the game, 56
    Knowledge, 55
    Officiating, 55
    Turkeys, 57
Commercial Logs
    Baseball, 41
    Basketball, 102-105
    Developing, 101
    Hockey, 49-50
    Volleyball, 53
Communication
    Board Operation, 20
    Non-verbal, 14
    Over-smile, 17
Constants
    Free Throws, 21
    Less than 5, 18
    Quick Recaps, 20
Credibility, 80
Crew
    One or Two Person, 11
Cues
    Non-verbal, 14

D
Dress Attire, 80

E
Eating, 22
Employee, 4, 8

F
Flow System, 79

G
Game Logs, 71
    Commercial

H
Highlights
    Game, 70
    Package, 78
Hobby, 4, 6
Hockey
    Goal, 47
    Layout, 46

I
Independent, 4, 7
Interviews
    Bad Questions, 23
    Good Questions, 23
    LIVE interviews, 109
    Parrots, 24
Intros
    Arch Story, 76
    Open, 75
    Pregame, 70
    Teaser, 74

Writing, 73

L
Live Copy
　1-5, 70
　Writing, 77

P
Play by Play 31
　Aircheck, 84
　Baseball, 39
　Building Focus, 38
　Coach Focus, 38
　Court Microphone, 107
　Criticism, 111
　Crowd Focus, 37
　Defensive Focus, 35
　Description, 29
　Dribbling Focus, 37
　Dual Role, 15
　Duties, 12
　Equipment, 97
　Errors, 20
　Exercises, 27
　Expectations, 85
　Extras, 108
　Football, 42
　Format, 106
　Foul Focus, 37
　Game Flow, 18
　Hockey, 46
　Interruptions, 21
　Media Timeouts, 107
　Measuring the Shot, 28
　Pass Focus, 37
　Personality, 17
　Promotion, 108
　Pronunciation, 17

Push-Pull, 100
Off-Ball Action, 33
Off-Ball Focus, 32
Off-Court Action, 19
Offensive Focus, 34
Reference Points, 19
Rundown Sheets, 107
Segmenting The Court, 31
Shot Clock Focus, 36
Shout, 106
Southern Accents, 22
Things to Do, 26
Things to Know, 25
Travel Focus, 37
Versatility, 109
Voices, 109
Voice Levels, 107
Volleyball, 51
Women v Men, 21

S
Sales
　Added Value, 91
　Appointments, 87
　Business Cards, 86
　Close, 91
　Comparisons, 95
　Decision-Maker, 88
　Face-To-Face, 90
　Friends, 88
　Follow-ups, 90
　Fun, 87
　Income, 94
　Inventory, 88
　Lazy, 91
　Listenership, 93
　Medium, 90

Money, 89
Organized Functions, 90
Phone, 87
Price Levels, 96
Price Points, 89
Pricing, 90
Rates, 89
Retention, 91
Sales Secret, 87
Sponsorship, 86
Tax ID, 86
Tire-Kickers, 89
Trade, 89
Show Prep
Art of, 22
Binder, 70
Postgame, 71
Sports Talk
Announcers, 60
Format, 59
Forum, 60
Producing, 60
Talent, 67
Topic Tree, 64
Sportscast Territory
Approach, 82
Buying Time, 110
Commercial Call, 82
Contact, 80
Plans, 81
Preparation, 110
Resume, 82
Territory, 83
Travel, 81
Sponsorship, 81
Statistics
Home/Visitor, 71

T
Target Market, 9
Men, 9
Middle Class Families, 9
Sponsors, 9

V
Voice
Care, 18
Lubrication, 19

W
Weekly Releases, 72

The Sportscaster's Notebook
by
Troy Kirby

Order This Book for a Friend!
ISBN 1438207204   EAN-13 9781438207209
Available on www.amazon.com

Made in the USA
Middletown, DE
31 July 2020

14079933R00066